STRAIGHT TALK ABOUT TEACHING
IN TODAY'S CHURCH

BOOKS BY LOCKE E. BOWMAN, JR.
Published by The Westminster Press

Straight Talk About Teaching in Today's Church

How to Teach Senior Highs

STRAIGHT TALK
ABOUT TEACHING
IN TODAY'S CHURCH

BY

LOCKE E. BOWMAN, JR.

The Westminster Press

Philadelphia

PUBLISHED BY THE WESTMINSTER PRESS®
PHILADELPHIA, PENNSYLVANIA

PRINTED IN THE UNITED STATES OF AMERICA

To my son, Locke III

CONTENTS

FOREWORD

When someone says there is a time bomb ticking, we should listen. When the explosive is nearby, we should beware. If what is nearest and dearest is threatened, we should do something. If we have time to check on who is warning us, we ought to ask whether he knows what he is talking about. We have all seen movies in which an expert is called to dispose of a dangerous bomb of one sort or another. The expert goes to work in a knowledgeable way to disarm the danger. The perspiration on his forehead suggests his care and precision. Every move is deliberate. His courage is shown simply by his being there and doing his job. When the threat is finally removed, there is usually some person or group to show enthusiastic gratitude for his skill and daring.

We should pay attention to the author of this book. He is not warning us of a bomb in the church out of ignorance or panic. He is a professional who knows the field of education as well as the Christian faith.

Pastors, decision makers, denominational educators, Christian education committees, and — above all — teachers, should be grateful for this book. It shows the way to deal with a real time bomb.

The Christian church universal is not doing its job at this moment in history in any creditable way. Herein lies the peril.

As you observe the work of this book's author, you realize he is a careful craftsman. His illustrations are not chosen for their shock value. He deals with the teaching church from a helpful point of view. He is very specific about problems usually ignored. He shows imagination as well as courage under the pressure of the moment. If the church must teach or die, this book becomes an invitation to live in a healthy, teaching community of faith.

This Foreword is written from the point of view of a pastor who has watched with growing concern the developments in Christian education on a local as well as a national level. There may be a difference of opinion as to why the prepared materials and helps fail to reach effectively the very people for whom they are prepared, but no one can deny that the community of faith is always just one generation away from extinction. Not to help teachers really to teach is risky.

The focus of this book is on the place where teacher, pupil, and community of faith meet. There is an excitement in the author's view of the teaching role in the church. Both American culture and the American church need to ponder what can be done in the light of Mr. Bowman's comments. Those responsible for recruiting, training, and encouraging teachers could share this attitude and help pass it along to the ones who learn through the teachers.

The gospel and its implications need desperately to be shared and thought through by this generation. Most of the wisest analysts and spokesmen for our time agree that we are in a new era. The post-modern world is moving so fast that the moral and spiritual values that went into the shaping of this new day could be overlooked with tragic consequences. "Teach now!" may not be too strong a way to put our prime responsibility. This is a book that begins to show us how.

The Arizona Experiment in Biblical Studies and Teaching, to which reference is made in this book, was witnessed firsthand by many of us here. Even to attempt it involved some risk. Sophisticated professional teachers as well as reservation Indians have benefited from watching how one can teach in today's church. It is one thing to prescribe and another to *demonstrate*. The latter has proved the most effective way to bring about creative change. The Synod of Arizona of The United Presbyterian Church in the U.S.A. is better equipped for meeting its responsibilities as a teaching church because this approach has been taken seriously. This man knows whereof he speaks.

PAUL DAVID SHOLIN

Tucson, Arizona
St. Mark's Presbyterian Church

PREFACE

No one could have convinced me fifteen years ago, when I was getting ready for my installation as a pastor, that I would someday become a zealot and pamphleteer in the field of church education. I wanted to be a pastor and preacher, and I was turning my back on a year in which I had been teaching at my alma mater.

But it was inevitable that I should slowly come to the conviction that the church's greatest need is for patient teachers. It began one day in our manse dining room when a Boy Scout (working on his God and Country Award) was sorting through some church bulletins that he had just helped me to mimeograph. Suddenly I heard him speaking reflectively about something I had taught him in a class two years before that. It astonished me that he recalled it. I thought, What an incredibly wonderful thing. I taught this fine boy something that has taken on deep meaning in his life.

Not long after that I was persuaded to resign as a pastor and to be installed as an editor of curriculum materials for my denomination. This brought me into contact with teachers who wrote letters and who sought me out at meetings around the country. I became fascinated with the problems of the volunteer church teacher. I remain so.

In 1965 I had the good fortune to be assigned a project in the field of teacher education. I traveled widely and interviewed dozens of teachers, then put many thoughts to paper. In August of that year I began my two-year stint with the Arizona Experiment in Biblical Studies and Teaching, a venture cooperatively undertaken by the United Presbyterian Church's Board of Christian Education and the Synod of Arizona. The reader of this book will find numerous references to the Experiment.

I have, in this latest period of my life, been facing two ways. As a national staff member, I know the problems of curricular development; I know how hard denominational leaders work to try to be useful to the parish ministry. But as an itinerant among the congregations, I have listened and heard plainly what the volunteer teachers' problems are. As the reader will discover in the pages that follow, I believe we face a crisis in our teaching ministry. Communication is lacking. Needs are severe. Most of all, the churches' decision makers are apathetic about teacher education.

I am grateful to my colleagues for all that they have taught me. Especially I am thankful for my Board of Christian Education, which gives me freedom of expression and encourages diversity of opinion. I hope this little volume of personal impressions, convictions, and observations will serve only to advance the ministry of teaching. It will surely do so if it sparks discussion — and all the more if it produces a bit of controversy.

L. E. B., JR.

Scottsdale, Arizona

CHAPTER 1

WHO WILL STAND AT THE TEACHER'S SIDE?

(An introductory challenge directed principally at the churches' decision makers)

Why is it that only a tiny minority of today's Christians give serious consideration to the subject of *teaching* in the church?

Clergymen are ambivalent; while all readily speak of teaching as important, most admit frankly that their busy lives allow little time for doing any, or for giving it concentrated attention. Parish decision makers may devote a day now and then to the general area of " Christian education," but seldom do they visit the scene where a teacher and pupils are at work. Few penetrating questions are asked about the quality of the teaching. Debate occurs occasionally regarding the choice of courses, scheduling, and curricular resources, yet the fundamental issue is displaced. That issue, simply stated, is: What kind of teaching should be going on among Christians today?

Great irony resides in our current situation. First, it is ironical that we should have invested so much money in recent decades for construction of church classrooms, while giving so little thought to what happens inside these newly built walls. Secondly, it is ironical that church publishers and educators should have invested so much time and money in devising printed educational materials, while lacking substantial empirical evidence of how these products are used and adapted. And it is ironical that our theological institutions have offered such outstanding resources to students, while their graduates exhibit only a token understanding of how to communicate theological concepts to other human beings.

But it is not this book's purpose to scold or lambaste. Far too much blame has been laid on today's pastors, church agencies, and theological schools, for any and all ills in Christendom. Our purpose is to lift up the words *teaching* and *teacher* and to plead for a creative, fresh approach to both.

There must be ways to increase teachers' competence. The times are urgent for doing so. Approaches not tried before on any wide scale will have to be devised and set quickly into motion.

GETTING OFF THE TRACK

No one in his right mind denies the significance of teaching. Even the most radical of the "radical Christians" who have created a theological stir recently would be slow to play down the role of teaching. Those who wrote of the "death of God" were themselves gifted teachers in noted institutions of learning. And surely all among us who retain our traditional ties to church and parish life recognize the New Testament basis for a threefold ministry of teaching, preaching, and healing. The quality of a Christian's spiritual and intellectual development is usually related to the kind of teaching made available to him throughout his lifetime. The teaching of the Holy Spirit, without which our lives are utterly barren, is a teaching mediated through servants in Christ's church. Teachers deserve honor, and our help.

So, there is little need to convince anyone that teaching really matters. It does, of course. The vexing problem is that even those specialists who have a vital concern about it are so easily diverted from examining the teacher's work at close range. We get off the track in several ways:

1. For one thing, many of us talk a lot about curriculum theory in almost total isolation from the classroom.

Theories are essential, and we must not deny their valid role in improving what we do. Some theories come before practice; others follow practice. But theory in a vacuum, without attention to how it really works out or gets revised, is of reduced value.

2. Similarly, we talk about Biblical and theological concepts in virtual isolation from the lives of parishioners.

Specialists in Bible and theology are seldom in close touch with the day-to-day problems of a volunteer parish teacher. This is not altogether bad. Progress in these fields of scholarship, as they are presently defined, would likely be impeded if the professors had to worry over details of parish teaching. It is probably unrealistic to expect these persons to be involved in elementary questions regarding classroom practice. Still, there are haunting questions we cannot escape: Who is responsible for interpreting the Biblical and theological specialists' ideas and discoveries? What skills are required of the interpreter?

3. Finally, the specialized field of " education " itself deflects us from thinking about teaching.

Too easily we shift our attention to stating " goals and purposes " in educational terminology, discussing such absorbing topics as " climate for learning," " supportive roles in the community," " motivational factors," and innumerable others. These abstract terms, not to be denied their proper place, belong to the descriptive language of technicians. But time and again they tend to prevent us from talking realistically about what a teacher *does*.

In thousands of active parishes, Christians by the tens of thousands are asked every year to " teach." We distribute to these persons a wide variety of materials and urge them to get busy at their jobs. Perhaps no more than one out of twenty of these volunteers receives personal counsel on a sustained basis regarding what he is to do when he works with pupils.

Regional or local training events are held periodically. For obvious reasons they tend to center on generalities. The enrollees study content-in-general, method-in-general, and the pupil-in-general. Thus, the proportionately few teachers who go to these special sessions find their note-taking of only minimal value when it comes to the hard reality of walking into a room and facing a group of pupils for a period of time.

Catch any random sampling of parish clergy and ask them what they think about Christian education. Candidly they reply that it is a puzzling area of specialization which they have never had the time to check through with any degree of thoroughness. Not that they are against it, or hostile toward it. It is simply a field they regard as jargonized and hard to pin down.

So-called senior pastors in churches with multiple staffs often speak possessively of " their " directors or other subordinates who take charge of the educational programs. Talk with enough of these directors, and their most frequent complaint is: " My minister doesn't really understand my problems. We never talk about my work."

It is hard to locate outspoken pastors who exhibit a passionate, personal concern for the ministry of teaching.

Where they do, they often fail to keep up with the periodic homework that would put teeth into their statements of support for classroom teachers. That is to say, they neither take nor have the time to find out *what* is being taught and *how*. (The foregoing sentences are not so much critical allegations as mere statements of fact.)

This relative indifference is what has to be changed. We need a revolutionary involvement of lively, respected spokesmen in the Christian community who will plead with clarity for a fresh attack upon the problems of the teacher. Something like what happened in the civil rights movement needs to happen all over again in the field of the church's teaching ministry. Many clergymen and laymen struggled as a lonely minority for decades, trying to bring the spotlight upon racial injustice. Still, not much happened beyond token involvement as far as the church on the whole was concerned. But what was the result when prominent clergymen — big name leaders and bishops — began to be arrested and to speak unequivocally? Everyone knew then that the church was truly engaged in the struggle. Let us hope it remains so.

Is it too much to hope that the respected, authoritative voices of the church's leaders may be enlisted to bring similar impetus to a crusade for better teaching among Christians? Nothing short of some such dramatic occurrence is likely to command the equal attention this subject surely deserves.

Four Points of View

As indicated earlier, diverse matters have prevented vitally concerned personnel from giving attention to the teacher's work. How much more easily diverted are the rest of us! We have drifted into thinking that someone, somewhere, is dealing with the teaching task and that we can leave it to his capable hands. This is a form of drifting that will bring dire consequences before too many more years.

There is a time bomb in the Sunday school — and that is the lack of trained teachers. Sunday school is likely either to be given up as a lost cause or to explode and die. Neither of these occurrences would necessarily be a disaster if we had something significant to offer in the Sunday school's place. Without a better system to supplant them, the death of Sunday classes would be very sad. Again, all too little thought is being given to plausible alternatives for making good use of teaching times in the church.

We must look at the entire constellation of problems clustering around the church's teaching ministry from at least four points of view. Let us make a very sketchy attempt at this:

First, consider the *pupil* of today — any person from the nursery on up the age brackets. What are his general educational experiences likely to be? He has the reasonable expectation of attending a public or private school where the very best resources are at hand for helping him to learn. Large amounts of money are spent to supply good buildings, good books, and handsomely appointed classroom settings. One has to travel far to come upon an American classroom unaffected by the current revolution in education. Teaching is not uniformly good, and many teachers lack basic skills. Yet, on the whole, the quality is improving. For all our criticism of them, the school setups in our society are outstanding. Learning can be a highly exciting business as teachers employ more and more new techniques to bring their pupils into a creative engagement with ideas and ways of thinking and problem-solving.

Let any pupil walk out of his public school classroom and over to his nearby church classroom. How do the rooms compare, to his way of thinking? What are the differences?

Just for enlightenment on this score, try surveying the churches of any neighborhood to see how many elementary and secondary classrooms are equipped with good chalkboards or suitable substitutes. Find out how many of them are actually used regularly by teachers. The survey will appall any serious observer of church teaching. And this sort of observation will not escape the pupils. Children are well aware of the sharp contrasts between their weekday schooling and what happens in church settings.

When queried about the quality of his church's teaching, a typical eleven-year-old responded recently: "The teacher spends most of the hour telling us to be quiet while we sit there wondering what we're supposed to do."

From the pupils' point of view, the church teaches less engagingly and with less of a sense of direction than does the public school.

Think next of the *trained leadership* in the denominations — professionals in church education. What viewpoint determines their general picture of teaching?

Preoccupied with manning the battle stations — with recruiting enough people to keep the enterprise going — they are not always cognizant of the minute problems of maintaining quality. But granted a real concern on their part, they may be understandably anxious about how to pump new life and enthusiasm into a teaching staff. Literature in the field is wordy and evasive, with few prescrip-

tions offered. Denominational specialists have had their
energies channeled into administrative chores; they are
left precious little time to live with parish leaders' practical problems and to supply helpful counsel.

Professionals have laid heavy stress in recent years upon
flexibility in all curricular materials and parish planning,
but flexibility can be a dodge for avoiding specific, concrete tasks. Flexibility as an ironclad principle is suspect,
for it runs counter to nature. Nothing very creative is
achieved with these flexible instruments. What is called
for is a variety of specific items, each with its own hard-
ened and well-tested form. Then choices can be made by
the teacher and planner; we choose the tested, workable
ideas that are suitable in our given parish setting. If each
curricular item is impotently flexible, seeming not to have
been fully formed in anyone's mind, then we have reason
to protest and reject.

Many pastors and directors in the church indicate personal confusion about how to make use of resources and
services provided for them by their denominations. Feeling thus, and not quite knowing how to plead their case
constructively with appropriate authorities, they let the
problem of teacher training await some future day's turning. Volunteer teachers come and go, but sustained dis-
course on precisely how they are to do their jobs is actually neglected by the army of professionals.

Arrayed between the pupils and the professionals are
the valiant volunteers who are doing most of what the
church calls teaching in our time. They are the ones who
need a sympathetic ear, and by whose side we all should
stand. From the individual *teacher's* point of view, the di-
lemmas are great.

Today's volunteer teachers are often the busiest people in the world. They are caught up in dozens of community and church activities, and they look askance at anyone who suggests several hours' preparation for each hour of classroom labor. The time is unavailable.

Many are teaching out of a sense of duty, purely. ("Someone has to do it, so I'll serve my turn.") A large percentage remain unconvinced that church teaching has long-lasting significance.

Despite the foregoing, our churches' teachers are heroic. Their plight sometimes drives them to tears, and they must weep alone, for they can seldom count on any reliable form of sympathetic support as they carry out their work.

The problem of equipment alone is staggering. Many a congregation builds a structure to house its classes, failing to appropriate an adequate sum for equipment. Old chairs and tables, and junky pianos and cabinets, are transferred into the new quarters. The teacher, with little or no guidance on how to improvise in such circumstances, is once again involved in an uphill struggle. Where this is the case, any vision of a fresh start in a well-furnished classroom comes to naught.

Curriculum materials are often ordered and distributed on a spotty basis. As likely as not the teacher may find he has too many of some nonessential items and only a single copy of a "must" piece. Then there is the perplexing business of finding one's way around in the teaching guides. At times this may take on the aspect of searching through the yellow pages of a phone directory; the number of cross-references becomes a frustration rather than an aid to the user.

Teachers observe their pupils displaying the ill temper

and boredom of boys and girls forced by parents to attend classes against their will. Others, for reasons not quite clear, are simply recalcitrant and rebellious. How to adjust to the needs of all these children is often more than a job for a professional psychologist.

Can the volunteer handle such a multiplicity of problems?

Over and over, the men and women who struggle to teach in our churches give voice to a common refrain: "What *is* a good classroom situation? How is a teacher supposed to perform?"

Finally, we have the *parents* of our congregations. In recent decades every major denominational agency for education has applied all the energy it could muster to propagandize for parental involvement in church education. The post-World War II push in the direction of church-and-family cooperation was eclipsed by the appearance of television sets in every home. Throughout the fifties, America readjusted its patterns of family living to accommodate hours of video. All that leisure time the church had counted on, during which presumably the parents would be sharing their Biblical and theological knowledge with their children, was suddenly preempted by this engrossing pastime.

What do the average parents expect the churches to teach? Soberly they defer to the church almost total responsibility for religious instruction of their children. This is not wholly to parents' discredit. They recognize their own inabilities and gaps in training, and they welcome the church's programs for helping their children to learn.

Beyond that, not much more can be said. Parents generally do not conceive of church school attendance in the same way in which they regard their children's attendance at public school. Many fail to sense how disruptive and discouraging it can be to a teacher when pupils attend spasmodically and miss vital links in units of study.

Any kind of homework assignment is likely to be ignored or resented. Parents have not thought that a voluntary church school system should require that sort of involvement.

In summary, the usual family household in the congregation takes church school for granted. It is an important opportunity that will always be provided, but it is more like a service we can subscribe to when we wish (as one would plug in to a public utility). No ground swell of understanding on the part of parents has yet appeared. Most of the fathers and mothers in our time would be surprised to hear that teaching presents any real problems to the church. They are out of touch with what is happening.

Take all these points of view together, and they add up to a single conclusion:

We lack any generally accepted image of church teaching. Neither pupils nor parents, neither professionals nor volunteers, have arrived at any consistently clear picture of a functioning teacher-pupil relationship in the church. The image actually grows fuzzier year by year.

WHERE TO BEGIN

Is the situation capable of redemption? Are there any strategies to suggest?

Plainly, the line of attack should be at the classroom level. Prolonged attention by theorists, theologians, Bible scholars, professionals, and anyone else whose interest can be aroused should be given to what happens in a church classroom — where someone called a teacher is at work with pupils. For if we cannot give practical expression to our ideas about teaching, if we cannot demonstrate empirically just what we mean by " good " teaching, and if we cannot arrive at consensus on what a volunteer teacher can be expected to achieve, then we really have church education nowhere except on paper or as a figment of someone's imagination.

The teacher has been imposed upon, criticized from lofty vantage, and generally left to sink or swim. This has gone on long enough. Now is the time to stand at the teacher's side and face his problems from the word go.

We cannot devise adequate curricular materials in isolation from the classroom. They cannot be planned realistically without a classroom teacher at hand through every stage of their development.[1]

We cannot recommend equipment and environmental arrangements apart from actual involvement in the logistics of classroom operation.

We cannot plan teacher training programs in settings that are only abstractly related to the week-by-week teaching situation, that is, the normal parish conditions familiar to the trainees.

We cannot afford the luxury of a large number of trained Christian educators whose energies are dissipated by chores that have little to do with what happens in the classrooms. At present, it is no exaggeration to point out that many professional church educators function quite acceptably without ever entering a classroom of the parish. They can also operate quite acceptably, by present standards, without ever doing a thorough reading of their denominational curricula. The administrative tasks attending their jobs, the time-consuming problem of recruiting personnel, and the endless rounds of local, regional, state, and national meetings of committees and other consultative groups, to say nothing of ecclesiastical meetings at which attendance is required, leave them with more than ample justification for neglecting the classroom.

Few denominational leaders have faced up to this shocking disconnection between professionals and the church classroom. Let the truth be stated once for all: hardly anyone except the teachers and pupils really knows what is going on; no one else is making it his steady business to find out.

Standing at the teacher's side involves three separate stages:

First, we must be at hand as he *prepares* for a typical study session with his pupils. What kinds of knowledge are absolutely essential before he can enter the classroom with competence and turn in a creditable job?

Startling as it sounds, we cannot take for granted that today's church teachers are uniformly able to locate a Bible reference cited in a teaching guide. (When, for example, a group of teachers were queried about this, they confessed they were not sure what to make of such citations as these: Col. 3:13b and Matt. 6:1-15; 7. The *b* after 13 was especially troublesome. The fact that a semicolon after the 15 meant a shift from the fifteenth verse of ch. 6 all the way over to ch. 7 was detected by relatively few.)

Terminology such as " exegetical " and " epistolary material " and " eschatological writing " and " apocryphal text " frequently crops up. Only a few initiates know what to do with such references, and even a standard dictionary is not always directly helpful.

Standardized expressions used by educational experts seldom carry very much freight for the untrained volunteer. An excellent example is "interest center," so often used in kindergarten and primary guides of all kinds. (In one classroom, a teacher had done her best. She had set up a card table with a poster above it. On the poster were the words "Interest Center," and on the table was a collection of sundry items ranging from starfish to *Life* magazine.) Just as many a cook cannot picture how a foreign recipe is likely to turn out, so our volunteer teachers lack the ability to read teaching guides and grasp mental images of an interest-centered kindergarten room. This is *not* a fault of the teacher; it is, instead, the result of an unrealistic expectation on the part of curriculum writers.

Small wonder that teachers protest a lack of Biblical knowledge and a dearth of pedagogical know-how. No one has walked patiently alongside them at the planning stage.

Second, we must be around to examine the teacher's *performance in the classroom* . . . both his strong points and his weaknesses.

Every teacher has his peculiar difficulties to overcome. He may do a splendid job of learning the pupils' names and establishing a friendly atmosphere. Or he may have a special knack for listening attentively to the pupils. But he may be woefully inexperienced at asking questions and leading a discussion to some logical conclusion. Or he may demonstrate no appreciable ability to make use of visual devices of various kinds. He may master the content of a portion of the Bible and yet see no point of contact between the concepts in it and the daily experiences of his pupils. Or he may draw the wrong conclusions from a

Biblical text because of inadequate attention to other related passages.

The point is that no one can improve his skills as a teacher if he is continually thrown entirely on his own resources and never has the advantage of observing superior teaching being done with pupils like those with whom he is to work.

We shall not get far in establishing criteria for teacher performance if we have no realistic data to go on.

Suppose we require, as one criterion, that a teacher must demonstrate skill at leading discussion. Is this a realistic expectation of all volunteer teachers? What kinds of experience would be required of a person before he could acquire such a skill — for sure? The plain truth is that we lack sufficient knowledge of where the teachers' troubles lie. We have spent too little time observing, taking accurate notes, and facing the real facts.

Large numbers of our teachers have strong points we can commend; their weaknesses stand out because hardly any personal counsel has been supplied for their benefit. The counsel can come only from someone who has learned by experience and who can put what he knows into simple terms.

Third, we must be available as the teacher *looks back* at what he has done and decides what value to place upon it. (This is a simplified definition of the overjargonized "process of evaluation.")

Not many of us have an inborn capacity to think over our accomplishments or failures and begin to pinpoint the reasons for them. Sometimes we succeed and really do not know why. At other times we fail and place the blame where it does not belong.

Better teaching demands a cultivated ability to retrace one's steps and analyze each one. We have to figure out what was worth doing and what was not, and *why* in either case.

What can we do to assist a volunteer in evaluating his work? An abstract evaluation form, devised and printed for him to fill out with pen or typewriter, is not the answer for everyone. A chance to talk things over with other teachers periodically may be a clue. But here, as in all aspects of a teacher's life, we need to fix our attention squarely upon the classroom. Materials and equipment are only part of a larger problem. That problem is a more suitable *image* of what we have a right to expect from a typical teacher in a church classroom.

(It may be that our problem is a failure to stress uniqueness in the church's teaching. Could it be that classrooms themselves are nonessential? Are there ways of supplying instruction to children and youth which would be markedly distinct — in atmosphere and technique — from what goes on in the public school? If so, what form, what style, would they embrace? This type of questioning is virtually nonexistent today. We have already opted for an "educational" system in our churches. That being the case, it is all the more imperative that we improve our classroom teaching. If we are irrevocably committed to going down that path, then we can at least go with devotion and thoroughness.)

PRIMARY ISSUES

Two obviously related factors have befogged any efforts to bring classroom performance into sharpest focus in our churches.

For one thing, every major denomination still takes a

highly centralized approach to curriculum materials production. In a board or other national department, a group of highly skilled professionals and an editorial staff turn out the materials. No matter how vigorously they protest their dependence upon writers from the local scene, the end result is invariably highly colored by the centralized procedure. Manuscripts are circulated among national staff members, and many revisions occur right up to press time. What often happens is that these staff members, through no intentional error on their part, fall into the habit of writing *for one another* rather than directly for their "consumers," the classroom teachers.

National denominational executives located strategically throughout the country are continually aware, as they must be, of their responsibility to promote the use of centrally planned materials. Although they are closer to the actual users, they still look primarily inward toward the church's national structure rather than outward toward the practical problems faced in the classroom.

There must be a healthy division between central and local planning in the church.[2] The production of resources for teachers may be one area in which this division has not been taken seriously.

As a direct consequence of this centralized production of materials, a second impediment to our efforts to produce better teaching is the fact that few curricular resources are fully *tested* in a variety of classrooms before they are published. And where testing has occurred, it has been done by professionals or semipros, often by the writers rather than by typical users.

No perfect "lesson plans" can be published. But it seems incredible that so many publishers persist in turning out attractive materials which have not, in fact, been used by anyone in just that form. The problems teachers will encounter will be first-time problems in all too many instances, all because time and money and skill were not turned toward providing genuine prepublication testing.

The time bomb in the Sunday school ticks away. More and more churches report grave difficulty in recruiting people to teach. Denominations report furtively to one another that church school enrollments are not keeping pace with the population. Actually, they are declining. A valid reason for these signs is surely our lack of focus upon helping the teacher to do a job to which he can give himself with pride. He will not wait much longer, for he senses that he is being asked to do a thankless task in all too many of our parishes. He senses also that the massive apparatus of professional church education is too far removed from the practical realities of his situation. He may be inarticulate about it, but he knows what others have only begun to suspect:

At present, few persons are standing sympathetically at his side.

CHAPTER 2

MAKING THE MOST OF WHAT WE ARE
(A preliminary attempt to take stock of the teacher's job, and the patterns of logic he must master)

The teaching done in the church is qualitatively different from other teaching to which we are exposed in a lifetime. This difference lies mainly in the fact that it is un-
deniably hortative. That is, the church yearns over us. She
voices an earnest hope that our lives will be personally af-
fected, that we will take new directions, because of our
participation in study and our receptivity to instruction.

Public school teaching possesses a similar quality at
times, when especially dedicated teachers seek to inspire
their students to deeper commitment, either to the goals
of our nation or to the personal values of better scholarship. In the church, this note of urgency is always there.
How to respond to it, with effective teaching, is one of our
problems. We could easily get the idea from some of the
popular evangelists and writers that we are to press our
students to make decisions at every possible opportunity;
often there is the implication that a teacher must prescribe what those decisions should be.

It is at this very point that we find most of our difficulties arising when we try to set forth a picture of improved
church teaching.

For example, a kindergarten teacher will sometimes exclaim, "It's so hard to keep their attention for an hour!" Upon closer inquiry we find her at work in a room filled with chairs. She has tried to keep fifteen or more four- and five-year-old children sitting quietly while she does a variety of things like storytelling, leading in "memory work," leading in singing, and generally trying to command their unswerving attention. Why does she do it this way? Why is she reluctant to let the children move about and learn in a room thoughtfully arranged to fit in with their interests at this age? She seems to feel compelled to work as she does because of her conviction that the church is a place to be serious, a scene for exhorting and seeking strenuously to "get across a message."

This teacher is more right than wrong in her basic position. The church does have serious business to do. It does have a message. Children need that message very early in life too. And kindergarten can be a fine place to convey what the church alone can say: God in Jesus Christ loves and keeps us.

But the teacher is badly off base when she thinks a roomful of young children can be fully attentive for an hour while sitting on straight chairs. Perhaps some of them can and will. Most will be a sad disappointment to her, week in and week out.

How can we persuade our kindergarten teacher that there is a better way to do her job, a way that will not require the sacrifice of one single bit of her zealous sense of purpose?

We have to begin by helping her to glimpse the thoroughly Christian idea that what we *are* in relation to young children is probably of far greater significance than any sentence carefully composed and spoken. In a kindergarten room where children have some freedom to speak and be themselves, the teacher has an opportunity to be herself too. She can be a good and responsive listener, a sympathetic friend who joins in the joy of their play or who shares their anxieties in a reassuring way. The love of God in Christ can be conveyed in a thousand ways in a relaxed, happy classroom. At no point does everyone have to sit on a chair in order for teaching to take place. Stories are told (and retold) and songs are sung — when the occasion is right; and a sensitive, listening teacher can learn how to sense almost intuitively when the right moment is there.

Teachers apparently feel all the more compulsion to talk their way into the minds and hearts of pupils who are at the older age levels. Having decided in advance what their pupils need, they concentrate on how to speak persuasively. It comes as a sad revelation that the pupils do not always listen and sometimes actually rebel.

Many junior high school pupils in the church begin to drop out from class attendance. Those who remain often include a number of boys and girls who have closed their minds to what the churches' curricula hope they will see, hear, and reexamine. Why? Because they have been " talked at " for so long that they think the church's classroom is devoted to one-way communication; the teacher speaks, and they listen. That is a pattern that has been increasing in intensity through eight or nine years of their lives.

Again, let us hasten to say that volunteer teachers are not villainous perpetrators of a bad situation. Neither are the pastors who also, for the most part, take a talk-oriented approach to teaching. No one is the villain. It is just that there has been no concerted effort to find out why teaching-by-talking is so ineffective, and especially ineffective in the latter third of the twentieth century. (A hundred years ago, it was more often true that the teacher talked and pupils listened, in school and church alike. Not so in today's good schools; we have better ways of working.)

The volunteer teacher who is honest often expresses dissatisfaction with his performance after a class session in which his own voice has been the principal sound throughout the hour. He knows something is missing. He hasn't been free to be himself in this situation. He doesn't quite know why.

He needs to hear again that the form and substance of all teaching in the church should be derived from a quite frank recognition of what the teacher *is* and what the pupils *are*. This is true because the Christian knows himself to be only what God, by his grace, has granted him in the way of talent and vision. We are what we are because God is who he is.

How can we help large numbers of teachers to change their images of the roles they play — to free themselves from the artificiality of what they are now doing? How can we retain our worthy hortatory concerns, as Christians who want our pupils to know Christ, and yet employ classroom techniques of a different order from mere talking or pleading?

PATTERNS ESSENTIAL

What we must all recognize is that we are incapable of communicating anything of lasting value without employing a pattern of logic.

In teaching, we are seeking to bring facts, generalizations, attitudes, appreciation, and skills or abilities into focus so that our pupils grasp them, make them their own, and keep them usefully at hand. We must adopt a systematic, orderly procedure in order to accomplish this. The pupils must be involved in doing things, reacting to ideas, and having experiences. There are logical ways in which the teacher can bring subject matter and pupil together, and the encounter is more likely to be memorable when this logical planning has occurred.

Volunteer teachers, unacquainted with or inexperienced in the *logic* of their jobs, will sometimes confess to a feeling that curricular materials are composed of many pieces of information and many discursive ideas simply " strung together." They read the lesson plans dutifully, but they fail to see any pattern other than that of " a string of beads."

So here is a teacher who leads her fifth-grade pupils in a brief Bible study, then tells a story from a curriculum guide, then requests her pupils to work at an " activity " that she has planned. The pupils see no connection between the parts of that hour's instruction, and this is no surprise to their teacher. She saw no connection either. It was just a string of beads. Why?

Although there may be many ways to help a teacher grasp the need for systematic planning and execution of an hour with pupils, it seems especially beneficial to dwell on the *deductive* and the *inductive* approaches.[3]

To deduce is to " lead or draw out from." The deductive approach is the oldest form of teaching. In using it the teacher states a principle, a law, or a generalization. Then he proceeds to give some illustrations of this statement. The pupils are then involved in analyzing the examples and in searching for other examples, possibly out of their own experiences. Thus the teacher begins the procedure by stating what he himself has discovered or found to be meaningful. The task before him is to move outward into the lives of the pupils; by citing examples and then supplying means for them to find and state new examples, he leads out from the general to the specific.

We can put this deductive procedure even more simply. It is like a cone:

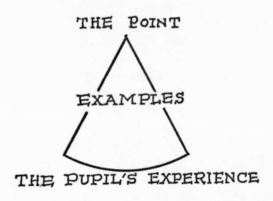

We start with "the point" — the main idea we seek to teach our pupils. Then we move outward and down to the broad base where our pupils live their lives. This can be a very effective way of teaching; it has worked for centuries, ever since Aristotle formulated it. The only problem is that we must be sure we are starting from a point that is true and relevant. It is quite possible to have an erroneous idea and to support it quite successfully by this procedure.

The other method of teaching is inductive. To induce is "to lead on" or "to tow." When we teach by this method, we begin with the observations of the pupils. They scrutinize the facts and problems surrounding a given topic. They and the teacher together develop some guidelines for searching out additional facts. Through these observations and research the procedure narrows down to a statement of laws, principles, or generalizations. The movement is just the opposite from that of the deductive procedure. The teacher employing the inductive method must begin with his pupils' experiences and bring them into some kind of focus so that, once summarized and fully examined, they supply a general truth which can be stated for careful study (and revision when new truth supplants it).

This procedure, too, can be simply put. It is like a funnel:

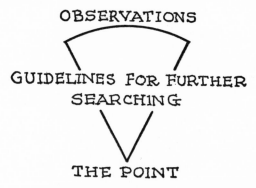

We start with what the pupils have seen and heard and felt. Then we look all around for the other things to examine — things that may tell us more. Finally, we narrow our focus until we have centered upon a point for emphasis — a logical conclusion based upon observation. This can be a most exciting way of teaching. Men have found it so ever since it was set forth as method by Francis Bacon, three and a half centuries ago.

LEVELS AND TYPES

It is not always an easy matter to determine whether we are primarily disposed toward an inductive or a deductive way of teaching. The problem is that we can discuss the inductive vs. the deductive methods on three separate levels. We must be clear as to which level we have in mind.[4]

First, there is the broad, general level of what we might call the process of church education. For some thinkers, the process begins with the *content* — the Bible, church history, and theological formulations. The presentation of this content is followed (or accompanied) by appropriate references to contemporary life and the problem situations facing the students. Other thinkers believe the process begins with some kind of analysis of the students' own *situation*, their preferences, needs, and experiences. From this point of departure, the movement of teaching is toward an eventual introduction of Biblical, churchly, theological material.

Often we find ourselves arrayed in camps — the " content " people (deductive thinkers) and the " person-centered " people (inductive thinkers). Before one can even start to work with a group of teachers, he can usually catch overtones of this problem with respect to process. And the teachers tend to cite examples proving the validity of their personal preferences:

Here is a teacher who begins by leading students into a book of the Bible, and this study germinates a surprising amount of concern about social witness. " See how it works! We began with Scripture and we were led to be actively in mission. That's the process."

But here is another teacher who faces the students to ask what they're really concerned about. Someone says, " About the problems of our city! " The others go along. So the group explores the city, and slowly they are introduced to specifically Biblical views about our mission in today's society. The teacher says: "Look at how it goes! We began with our life situation and we were led later into forms of Bible study. That's the process."

What happened here is not difficult to analyze. Each of the teachers, largely on the basis of personal preference, has chosen a way of working. One moved deductively, the other inductively. Each process is an inverted version of the other.

Second, there is the more specific area of curriculum *materials*. Here, too, the inductive-deductive preferences come into play.

The writers of "lesson plans" make deliberate choices as to the way a class session will begin. Sometimes the choice is essentially deductive-theoretical; at other times, it is inductive-empirical.

One lesson starts off with a Bible-reading assignment, then proceeds to supply the teacher with possible deductions that may be elicited from the students. The teacher is advised to lead the students in considering how these deductions relate to their own lives. (A few examples are given.) Some teachers will applaud this lesson's structure: "The Bible study led us into a lively discussion!" Others will say, "This lesson flopped — we couldn't get the pupils interested in the Bible at the beginning."

On the other hand, another lesson depicts some present-day life problem to be shared with the students and discussed. The problem itself leads to a generalization. This, in turn, leads to a period of study on a Biblical passage that is clearly related to that generalization. The procedure has been a matter of controlled induction. The curriculum material controls the inductive reasoning by presenting a specific current problem similar to life as the students know it. Presumably it is the kind of problem they themselves might voice.

Some teachers using this latter lesson will say: "That one really worked! It's best to begin where the pupils are." Others will protest negatively: "This isn't a good plan. There wasn't enough Bible in it, and I couldn't figure out the point."

(NOTE: It is highly important to distinguish between this controlled curriculum procedure and the much wider area discussed as general process above. A teacher's view of the total process of teaching will tend to govern choice of curriculum materials. His view of the teaching procedures within the curriculum materials themselves will strongly affect his evaluation of them.)

To repeat, it is largely the teacher's preference that determines what happens in the use of prepared curriculum materials. The inductive-empirical teacher prefers moving from the present situation back into Scripture; the deductive-theoretical teacher prefers beginning with Scripture and moving forward into the present life situation.

A third, even more specific area is that of *technique* employed in the classroom. In the final analysis, this may be the most crucial level. The inductive or deductive preference of a teacher tends to determine how he leads his students to examine a concept or topic.

Let us consider four teachers — two who begin their study sessions with Bible study and two others who begin with a life situation:

THE BIBLE STUDIES

Teacher A: He gives his students a number of resources such as commentaries, wordbooks, and mimeographed outlines. He assigns a Bible passage and suggests that they look it up in the commentaries, examine key words in the wordbooks, and consider how the passage has been outlined by others. Then, he leads the group in summarizing what they have discovered. (This is plainly a deductive approach to Bible study. It begins with generalizations already formulated by other students of the Bible, and the pupils engage primarily in retracing those steps. They reason deductively. Only occasionally will they raise questions about what others have deduced.)

Teacher B: He asks the students to read the Bible passage. He questions them carefully concerning what it says, what it means, how it all fits together, and what problems of interpretation it presents. Only after he discerns that they have exhausted their own resources for understanding what has been read does the teacher present to his pupils the commentaries, wordbooks, and outlines. They use these to look up what they could not figure out for themselves. (This is inductive Bible study. The students are required to move inductively, from their own observations, to consider the observations of others [in printed aids and in comments from a skillful teacher]).[5]

THE LIFE SITUATION

Teacher C: He describes in detail a situation in which a family struggles with the problems of poverty. Then he distributes pamphlets, a filmstrip, a recording, and a series of news clippings to the students. He asks them to formulate some statements on what may be done for this family through agencies and programs now in operation. Through the deductive technique, reasoning from data in their hands, the students prepare reports on how the family's difficulties may be resolved.

Teacher D: He speaks of the persons in a family unit, assigning names to them and giving brief character sketches. Then he announces that they live in a two-room apartment and have an annual income of $2,500. He asks: What is life like for these persons? Why? How will they meet their needs? Through continued questioning and summarizing, he brings before the whole group everything they know about poverty and its problems. Even the word " poverty " comes from a student who brings it up, not from the teacher. Finally, through this basically inductive technique, the students may be introduced to pamphlets, clippings, and filmstrips — to look up what they did not already know.

Thus, we can see how it is not enough to distinguish between induction-deduction in respect to (1) the general process of teaching, or in respect to (2) the curriculum materials. We must also take into account (3) the teacher's classroom technique. And to complicate the matter further, we must add a final observation:

Teachers may be basically inductive or basically deductive on one or more of these three levels, but not so in the others. The best way to visualize how this works out is by diagram, as shown on the opposite page.

There may be other types, but these appear to be the most prevalent ones.[6] Following is a brief interpretation of the types:

Types 1 and 2: These are the least numerous. They have the tendency to see their work from a broader perspective.

Teacher	Process	Materials	Technique
Type 1	Inductive	Inductive	Inductive
Type 2	Inductive	Inductive	Deductive
Type 3	Deductive	Deductive	Deductive
Type 4	Deductive	Deductive	Inductive
Type 5	Deductive	Inductive	Inductive
Type 6	Deductive	Inductive	Deductive

They speak often of the need for a totally new approach to parish education, beginning " in mission " and with the needs observable in the community. If they use printed materials at all, they will choose those which are " person-centered " or " pupil-centered " or " relationship-oriented." But in their classroom technique they will vary sharply between inductive and deductive approaches. (NOTE: Most of these teachers have had formal training. Directors of Christian education often fall into Type 1, for they have been trained to work in this way. This may be a clue to some of their difficulties in communicating with pastors and with laymen as well.)

Types 3 and 4: These are the teachers who speak often of church teaching as proceeding from specific content peculiar to the heritage and experience of Christians. Nearly always dependent upon prepared curricular materials, they prefer the deductive type of lesson plan — the one that begins with Scripture or some other formulation; but when it comes to classroom technique, they may choose either the inductive or the deductive procedure. (Most pastors who teach fall into Type 3. Having been trained in seminaries by the deductive-theoretical method of European origin, they are most at ease in a straight deductive pattern.)

Types 5 and 6: These teachers, too, are firm in their commitment to a defined content as the starting point. Still, they choose the inductive type of curriculum materials because they believe these to be "more relevant" to the church of today. But in his classroom technique, Type 6 will employ the deductive procedure rather than the inductive. (Many perceptive laymen, facing the options, choose to be Type 6. The reason for this is simply that they lack the ability to be at ease with the questioning process required by the inductive technique in the classroom. They worry about how to do it, so they shy away from it.)

We must not conclude that one of these six types of teacher is *necessarily* better than the others. It is possible to suspend judgment, and we should do so. Very good teaching can occur in the classrooms of all six types.

Getting Somewhere

Every teacher must understand that significant teaching involves the pupils, and that it *gets somewhere*. It has a "shape" to it; it holds together. One teacher, noting the cone and the funnel as symbols of the two methods, made this remark about herself: "I think my teaching is a kind of hourglass. We start out with the pupils' experiences, and then we narrow down to a generalization. For a time I take a deductive approach, eventually widening out to include the pupils' contributions once again." This wise observation could be made concerning many effective teachers. It is quite appropriate, even necessary at times, to combine the methods in this way.

However, until a teacher is able to chart some kind of pattern in his work, and can begin to recognize what his preferences are; until his work in the classroom has a discernible logic to it, then he flounders. He is threading a string of beads, or talking without clear aim, or concentrating overtime — with mounting frustration — on "holding the pupils' attention." (This problem of attention-getting often takes care of itself when a teacher knows what he is doing with respect to bringing pupils and subject matter into serious engagement.)

The first priority for the beginning teacher is to get a clear picture of how to begin and how to conclude a period of instruction. Does he start with questions? Are they questions related to what the pupils can be expected to understand (from reading or from experience)? Then what does he do next? Will he proceed in the pattern of the funnel or will he prefer the conelike procedure?

Thinking over the logic of what he will do requires the teacher to decide basically what kind of approaches are most to his liking. He will soon discover that curricular materials prepared for his use need not be cast aside if the form in which they are written happens not to appeal to him. More often than not, he can simply turn the suggested teaching procedure around. (A frequent complaint is that "lessons are written backward." What the teachers mean is that the lesson writers worked in cone or funnel patterns which, from the readers' point of view, should have been reversed. There is no reason why a teacher should not make that shift in pattern for himself. It is far better and far more convenient than laying the material away and searching for a substitute!)

In short, we discover how our own minds work — and how we can best relate our thinking to that of our pupils. This is partly determined by training and background. But a workable teaching method can be acquired without long periods of formal study. We teach best when we find out what kind of thinkers we are and then make the most of our gifts.

To spend this much space on logic in our teaching must not be taken as a rejection of a certain freedom and openness which many persons would refer to as " following the Spirit's leading." To be sure, there are times for abandoning even the best of teaching plans. But abandon them for what? In order to be a better teacher! In order to follow sudden flashes of intuition — or to meet suddenly apparent needs expressed by pupils. However, these moments can be fully appreciated, perhaps only fully recognized, when they *are* interruptions of our prayerfully conceived plans. And even when, in freedom, we travel with our pupils down an unanticipated path, we do *not* do so without the use of human logic. There may be abundance of emotion and even mystical insight, but these welcome invasions of our consciousness are never fully divorced from something that went on before. This fact in itself brings logic into the picture: from pursuit of one idea, we were led to another.

It is most unfortunate that so much energy has been devoted in years past to the battles between so-called " content people " and " methods people." The worst of it is that there has been more sparring than real battle. Content people, concerned for correctness of understanding and for an abundance of sound learning, have snubbed the methods people as technicians or gadgeteers who only distract the teacher and pupil from getting at the heart of the issues; they claim that classroom techniques are frills, hardly essential if the teacher is immersed in his subject. Not so, say the methods people. They tend to counter with the argument that all the content in the world can be lost if the teacher takes no pains to employ good methodology in its communication.

This kind of sparring and name-calling is sad enough in public education. It becomes doubly painful in the church, because the arguments on both sides take on theological overtones like the Biblical issue of " faith " and " works." The content people in the church tend to impugn the faith of the methodologists. The methods advocates counter that the theologians don't really care about people.

We can surely do with less of this sort of arguing. Today there is much wider acceptance, by all concerned, of the necessity for innovative approaches to classroom technique with children and youth. In the church there is still too little attention given to better methodology in the teaching of adults. Study materials are almost universally colorless in format, by comparison with those prepared for younger pupils. Guides for teachers are flimsy, and the techniques are generally unimaginative. What prompts the decision makers to conclude that adults learn best without benefit of a teacher who has logical and varied plans for discussions and other forms of classroom involvement?

There should be no conflict over content and method. In fact, the mental separation of the two leads only to confusion on the teacher's part. It is not a natural procedure to think of one without the other. Yet we persist in doing so on many occasions. The very structure of theological seminaries' curricula sometimes encourages this. The teacher of homiletics (preaching) may be regarded as a methods man while the scholar of Bible is regarded as a content man, uninvolved in the problems of practical interpretation. The graduating student, unless he is wary of the trap, may express a certain impatience with the Bible. He cannot figure out how to preach from it, for he has thought separately of content and method. Some sort of integrative approach is needed, and in recent years more theological faculties are experimenting along this line.

Parish teachers who wonder how to get started on their own task in communication should spend as much time as they can spare facing one key question prior to every study period with their pupils: What is the main idea (the point) for this hour of work in the classroom?

Once this established purpose can be clearly stated, the next questions to face follow in this order:

a. What do the pupils already know about it? (Have they studied it before? Have they examined a closely related idea?)

b. What kinds of material do I have at hand that will help the pupils to get a clearer understanding of the main idea?

c. What will be the pattern, the organized way of working, in this hour? (Will I state the point at the outset, so we can work from there? Or will we come to the point at the end?)

OPENNESS IS BEST

We hinted earlier at the problem of prescriptive teaching in which the teacher decides in advance what the questions are and how the answers should be framed. His material may indeed have a logical structure, but it is artificial. It is imposed upon the pupils from a viewpoint that may not conform at all to their thought patterns and frames of reference.

For instance, a teacher recently drew a five-pointed star on a chalkboard, directing his pupils' attention to a series of five questions, one placed at each of the five points. The questions were, he said, ultimate questions to be faced by young persons desiring to establish a Christian home. With only slight pauses, he then proceeded to take up each of the five areas in a tone of admonition.

The teacher meant well. He wanted his students to have a device they could remember, something to recall mentally in the future. (They would carry away a star in their heads, and surely they would remember one or more of the written questions at the star's points.)

The problem was an old one: The pupils were not involved in thinking through the outline for what transpired. They felt no sense of responsibility for it; it belonged to the teacher alone. So they sat it out, waiting for the teacher to unfold the five-point prescription. Admittedly, it is far easier to criticize this teacher than it is to offer an alternative to his technique. But think of the possibilities available to him for putting a variety of problems and images of homelife before the pupils, either at the beginning or at the end of the hour of instruction. In small groups or even as individuals, the pupils might have been led into numerous avenues of thought, all related to the one theme: a Christian cares about the quality of life in his home.

Was this teacher really teaching, then? In a way, yes. In another way, no. For the communication was largely one-way — admonitory and prescriptive. Pupils were passive. Improvement in his technique could lead this deeply committed man to think of his teaching as a two-way, active affair. Pupils themselves would be ferreting the raw material for questions. The teacher would be summarizing from their discoveries. (Perhaps the five ultimate questions would emerge as he taught, perhaps not. But what did take place would belong to the pupils in a different sense.)

The volunteer teacher undoubtedly has difficulties in mastering this root problem of pattern-and-involvement in his classroom technique. He may tend to an impatience that he regards as quite legitimate. After all, he feels, he must urge his students to make basic commitments. Is there time, he wonders, for the procedures that seem so painfully hard to carry through?

There is far too much convincing evidence that pupils learn best through the nonprescriptive, open procedure — too much for anyone to ignore it. And the techniques for encouraging active pupil participation can be acquired far more easily than most volunteers realize. Everyone concerned with improving the quality of what happens in the church classroom should, therefore, give serious attention to the forms of teaching we have just examined. Aristotle put it well when he said that form and substance are "twinborn."

CHAPTER 3

CONCEPTS AND THE PURSUIT OF QUESTIONS
(A short expedition into human thought, a complex of mystery and delight)

Once a teacher is aware of his need for orderly, systematic procedures in his work, a second major hurdle is learning how to *think along with* his pupils. The stress is on thinking and then analyzing why our thoughts (and those of our pupils) have taken a certain turn. Why did we not think down some other track?

Church school teachers have a very special opportunity to engage in this kind of reflection, for the church's subject matter is meditatively conceived and it calls for a high degree of thoughtfulness — interior reasoning and contemplation. This is so because theology is a science (field of inquiry calling for free-ranging exploration, the most strenuous type of mind-stretching).

So we must not make the mistake of sliding over and around what our pupils are thinking. The volunteer who teaches in the church must have a chance to give careful attention to what we mean by the term " concept."

A concept is a basic product of human thinking. It is a generalization. The rise of armed conflict in Vietnam, for example, is a concrete fact — an experience encountered over and over in the daily news. But the Vietnam war is not in itself a concept; *war* (the general term) is.

An elementary task of the teacher is to help a student to arrive at concepts or to revise those he has previously held. If this task can be appreciated and mastered, it is readily recognized as the very substance of good teaching.

One of the encouraging developments in the education of teachers, in college and university courses, is the idea of micro (small) teaching. Reduced to simplest terms, this is a technique in which a practice teacher is asked to teach a single concept to one pupil. The young teacher's goal is to figure out how he may stimulate the pupil to learn one small bit of general knowledge.

Take, for instance, the elementary fact that red and blue, mixed together properly, produce the color known as purple. The micro-teaching assignment is to devise a way of communicating this to a pupil.

How does the teacher begin?

He might decide to show the pupil something purple, then ask: How do you think the color purple comes into being? (Would there be a way to separate the red and the blue?)

He might show the pupil something red and something blue, then ask: If these two colors were mixed, what color would we have?

Or he might hand the pupil a bottle of blue liquid, and a bottle of red, then let him experiment on his own until he came upon the discovery that a mixture of the two produces purple.

(One ingenious teacher hit upon the idea of supplying the pupil with a thin sheet of red tissue and a thin sheet of blue, then asking him to lay one over the other and hold the two up to a windowpane so that he could see purple as the light shone through.)

This one example of micro-teaching is sufficient to illustrate how useful a technique it can be. Hardly any concept we are asked to teach, no matter how simple it may seem at first hearing, can be communicated without some pre-liminary planning — some choice of alternative approaches. It is good for teachers to be forcefully reminded that noth-ing under the sun is truly simple beyond question. We need to appreciate all that is involved within every con-cept as it is formed and re-formed.

And it is altogether needful that we be reminded occa-sionally to break our thoughts (thought-blocks, we might say) down into all the pieces they are made of. If a child can be taught to write a sentence at a very early age, then he can be taught to produce a paragraph. And it is from paragraphs that themes are made. But the sentence re-mains absolutely basic. Many a student has matriculated in college still not too sure of his sentence-building power. This should never happen!

In the church we may be especially prone to take the big leaps in our thinking and speaking, forgetting all the single concepts that accumulate to make up what amounts to a paragraph of thought.

INVITATIONS TO THINK

A concept, once again, is an idea generalized from par-ticular instances. It is abstracted (that is, drawn out) from our study of the concrete. A conception is the product of reflective thinking.

The Scriptures frequently invite us to think and reflect. The church is distinguished as a people partly because we have taken thought regarding our primary allegiance, our firmest commitment. This kind of taking thought is not to be equated with the worrisome preoccupation Jesus warns against in the Sermon on the Mount (" Take therefore no thought for the morrow"). Rather, it is the kind of thought-taking Paul means when he says, "Think on these things."

The word "concept" has to do with language. We use language to speak of all that has meaning for us; such a thing as nonverbal communication exists, of course, but that is another phenomenon entirely. The Bible is composed of words, Jesus Christ himself is the Word, and there is no escaping the necessity of language. Even an unknown tongue requires interpretation in intelligible language. The sin of idolatry can lead to babbling tongues, as attested by the story of the Tower of Babel; and faithfulness in the Bible is virtually equated with clarity, an ability to articulate one's commitment: "I believe; help thou mine unbelief." Can one imagine two more articulate clauses to summarize the committed Christian's position under God?

A concept is a cluster of impressions brought into a whole. A concept is derived from a collective range of particular objects and happenings. Concepts develop slowly, usually through concrete experiences.

We help a concept to take shape through both positive and negative instances. When we see a house cat, we say to the young child, "Cat." But we may also have occasion to say, "This stuffed bear is not a cat." A considerable number of such assertions, both positive and negative, may be necessary before the child has a fixed concept of the house cat.

Practically all the major concepts we learned as children and now use as adults were already in existence within our culture prior to our arrival. So we do not have to form them; we acquire them by means of our relationships to things and people around us.

Because this is the case, teachers frequently have the job

of correcting erroneous concepts that have gained wide acceptance in the culture. Certainly, the church's teachers meet this problem again and again. For example, some Christians are troubled by an idea that recurs often in the church — the understanding that God is in charge of us by means of a predestined calendar. According to such a view, every little event in our lives was determined before we were born, and nothing can be done about it. This is a non-Biblical, mechanistic concept of predestination, one that could easily lead us into despair. But why is it so tenaciously held by some persons? Because it has been taught, communicated, impressed. It is easy to take hold of, easy to pass on to others — especially in a machine age. So it is not easily corrected. We strongly resist new concepts that are offered to supplant those derived from earlier experience.

Educators warn us that concepts involving long time lapses between an event and its consequences are especially difficult to develop. That is just the sort of handicap we face when we seek to communicate our heritage in the church of Jesus Christ.

A group of first- and second-graders were being introduced to the idea of the New Testament church by means of a study of the lives of Peter, Paul, and other apostolic leaders. The teacher had an advantage because one of the class members was a boy named Paul who knew that his name came from the Bible. The teacher and the pupils had a pleasant time trying to get the feeling of how long ago the Paul of Scripture lived. The story of how his life was changed by Christ made him seem closer in point of time.

Then the teacher attempted something too difficult for these pupils. He pointed to a poster on which he had lettered a sentence written by the apostle Paul, from the letter to the Colossians. He asked, " Who do you think wrote this sentence? "

A boy in the group replied, " I think you [the teacher] wrote it."

The pupil was thinking concretely and of a particular instance, as a second-grader still does much of the time. The poster before the class was something the teacher had written. The reply was quite correct from the boy's point of view.

The teacher was thinking abstractly and in a generalization; the sentence was written by the apostle Paul. (Hardly any adult would have answered as the young boy did. Adults are conditioned to think abstractly and in generalizations. Seeing the poster, they would have said, " That was written by Paul.")

But the reason for the foregoing example is to underline the fact that pupils are *learning*. Therefore, a teacher has to put himself alongside the pupil and think with him. (In the case of the poster and the second-grader, the teacher did just that. He said: " You're right. I wrote these words on this poster, but I copied them from the Bible. Who do you think wrote them so they could later be printed in the Bible? " The boy thought a while and asked, " Did Paul write them? ")

It is utterly essential, for the pupils' sake, that the teacher work patiently and thoroughly in helping to bring New Testament events and their continuing consequences into focus.

Curricular materials frequently demand of the teacher more than ordinary interpretive skill. Two examples are indicative of the problem:

The first is from a guide intended to aid the teacher of

first-, second-, and third-grade pupils. The Bible story for the day is Acts 11:27–30. The guide suggests: " After the story, point out that this is the first time the Bible mentions one church giving an offering to another church. Explain that ever since that time, Christian people have been helping those in need." [7]

We should take careful note of how much is involved, conceptually, in these two sentences:

1. The concept of the Bible as authority. (This is a generalization; an abstraction — since the Bible gives us an example, we follow it. But this is certainly not self-evident and not communicated with ease.)

2. The concept of the church as a universal. Not all young children can be depended on to have this idea. One Arizona eight-year-old continually compared every reference to the church with what she knew of " the church we went to in Amarillo, Texas."

3. The concept of an offering.

4. The concept of our helping others in need. " Christian people " is an abstract expression that must be interpreted and made specific.

These four wide-ranging ideas are related to the larger concepts of serving and sharing. It requires much listening, thinking, examining, to be certain that a classroom full of children have grasped their meanings.

A second example comes from the material prepared for a teacher of fourth-, fifth-, and sixth-graders. In connection with a study in I Chron., ch. 16, these directions appear:

" Ask, ' What do you think of when people talk about " glorifying God "? ' (Most grown-ups and children alike think in terms of praising God for his holiness and power in a formal service of worship.) Comment that although we indeed glorify God in worship, we also glorify him when we witness to others of God's mercy and power." [8]

Consider how many abstract ideas are present in that paragraph:

Holiness/power/formal service of worship/mercy of God/witness/glorifying God.

It requires all the imagination and creativity we are capable of summoning in order to deal with the Biblical concept of glorifying God. It is not impossible, though, if we really work at it.

Educators have been revising many of their ideas as a result of the work of Prof. Jerome Bruner, of Harvard University, who has theorized persuasively that nearly any concept can be taught in some meaningful form to any person of any age. Taken at face value, this theory would suggest that we can teach, in some meaningful form, the idea of " glorification " to a preschool child, but it requires great thoughtfulness to do so at any age.

Concepts must be stated and examined within meaningful structures. We cannot talk about worship, for example, without first understanding the church as a people. We cannot talk about the church as a people without some idea that God brings people together. We cannot speak of being brought together without considering why this gathering is different from all other gatherings. And so it goes.

Part of the time we can rely on the child's intuition to supply him with sudden breakthroughs so that he gives expression to more complex ideas. He does not have to be led by the hand through every tedious maze of thought involved in the ideas we are considering. For instance, a Navajo youngster who could speak only a few words of English, looked at a magazine picture of a mother and child and suddenly exclaimed, " Love! " This is an intuitive breakthrough. The teacher listens at all times for these occurrences in his classroom; often he merely continues from where the pupils arrive on their own.

The teacher in the church must listen to his pupils' thoughts, trying to fathom with a third ear what is going on in their minds. The only way such a third-ear approach can be cultivated is for the teacher to work out his own thoughts first; then he is free to listen. If we are not certain of the ground we stand on, we have trouble giving attention to our pupils' positions. Ordinarily, therefore, it is better for a teacher to choose a quite limited amount of instructional material, claiming it as his very own, than to do a skip and jump over much that he has not had time to assimilate.

USING ANALOGY

The time-honored device for clarifying a Biblical or theological concept is the *analogy*. The Bible itself is replete with analogies. They are employed to press home the relevance of divine truth.[9] (An analogy is a resemblance in some particular between things otherwise unlike.)

Think of the words of Jesus, " No man, having put his hand to the plow, and looking back, is fit for the kingdom of God."

He was not thinking or speaking literally of plowmen. His rich Hebraic heritage made him thoroughly at home with parables, and so were his listeners. He was employing a figure of speech that is essentially analogy. Here is a plowman who is looking back instead of ahead to the furrow. He is *like* a man in general; we all set our hands to tasks, and these should receive our wholehearted, forward-looking attention. This is especially so for a man who has committed himself to God. He ought not to look back, wondering if this commitment is the right thing or allowing himself to be lured by other attractions. He must look ahead with singular devotion — keeping in the pathway he has set for himself as one of God's persons. The Kingdom of God, like the field of a plowman, demands men who will stick to their jobs, eyes straight-fixed on the way ahead.

Suppose a class of sixth-graders, studying the New England Puritans, discovers that this saying of Jesus was a favorite with their stalwarts. We can ask why this might have been the case. To arrive at an answer, the pupils must think analogically. The Puritans themselves were like plowmen who never looked back; they kept the faith in their covenant community. To press the analogy, the teacher then asks: What does the saying suggest about our own lives in the community of Jesus Christ, *now?*

Teachers must have some drill and practice in the careful use of analogy. No analogy is totally satisfactory, of course; but without analogies, the teacher is impoverished.

We have to exercise care in selecting analogical material. One teacher who wanted to stress the disciples' need to be independent of Jesus' physical presence and to act in faith as his messengers (a legitimate point to make in New Testament study) chose a poor analogy. She said to her boys and girls: " It was like cutting the apron strings. You all know that, don't you? " As a matter of fact, they did not know this idea at all. So she was caught having to explain apron strings, and the whole purpose of the analogy was more or less lost in the process.

We have to reinterpret many Biblical analogies due to our radically changed frames of reference, but when we ourselves devise analogies, we should not have to explain in detail. One set of particulars in the comparison should be wholly familiar to the pupils — that is the test of a useful analogy.

FORMING QUESTIONS

In all our conceptualizing and reexamination of ideas, we must encourage the raising of countless questions with and among the pupils. Research among church teachers reveals that they tend to fear the raising of questions in the classroom, primarily because they do not think they are capable of controlling what would occur if the questions were allowed. In short, they fear the possibility of questions to which they themselves cannot frame adequate responses; hence, they shy away from asking questions of their pupils. This is a sad commentary.

The good teacher should desire questions to be raised. He can steer his way through those which are irrelevant and tangential, and without hurting feelings. Mainly, he is dependent upon these questions for bringing essential facts into the open, for a sounding board of what the students are thinking, and for giving clues as to where the discussion should lead next.

One interesting idea to try with older pupils is to assign a passage for them to read, supplying paper and pencils to individuals or to teams of class members. Then ask them to turn every factual statement into a question. Supplying a few examples on the chalkboard will help, such as:

Statement: The United States is in the northern hemisphere.

Question: In what hemisphere is the United States located with respect to the North and South Poles?

The questions prepared by the students themselves can

then become the basis for subsequent class discussion.

Every teacher has to learn this procedure of converting statements into questions. The good questions begin with a *w* or an *h*. They are: Who? What? Why? When? Where? How?

A way of impressing this question-framing habit upon the beginning teacher is to remind him repeatedly that questions fly up off the page as we read the Scriptures or any other written material. Behind every complete sentence is one or more questions.

As an illustration of the wealth of questions that may arise from a single line in the Bible, turn to Acts 6:1: " Now in these days when the disciples were increasing in number, the Hellenists murmured against the Hebrews because their widows were neglected in the daily distribution."

Here is a partial list of questions written out by one study group:

What is meant by " these days "?

Why were the disciples increasing in number? How long did this growth continue?

Who were the Hellenists? the Hebrews?

What is meant by " murmured against "? Was this the complaint of a minority group?

Who was considered to be a widow? What was her status in New Testament times?

What was being distributed daily? By whom? To whom? When? Why?

In the next verse we find a reference to " tables." What kind of tables were they? (Commentators do not all agree on this.)

Even a rather young child, hearing Acts 6:1 read aloud, can raise most of these questions. They are, after all, essential in order to interpret the line satisfactorily. Every teacher and curriculum writer must learn to construct suitable questions.

PROGRAMMED INSTRUCTION

Any discussion on the teaching of concepts would be incomplete these days if we overlooked an increasingly popular tool for occasional classroom use in the public schools — programmed instruction (the teaching machine concept). The technique is surrounded by a somewhat cumbersome terminology, but the principal notion behind it is that larger concepts are broken down into small learning steps. These are repeated in a variety of patterned arrangements, and the learner is asked to respond to every stimulus in some overt way (by writing or performing some other concrete act). The stimulus is a sentence or group of sentences called a program "frame." Within it will be a blank space or a question. The learner fills in or answers. Then at once he turns to see whether he wrote the correct response.

Sometimes, in a particular type of program, the learner who responds incorrectly, or in some particular way, will be referred back or forward to another frame. This is done to help him correct his error (through repetition or remedial work) or to speed up his pace if he gives evidence of superior knowledge. Such a procedure is called "branching."

We learn at least two very helpful things from programmed instruction as a technique. One is the value of having to break down what is to be taught into all the logical small steps so that the learner is left in no doubt as to how one idea relates to another. The other is something we have always known but have not always practiced: Meaningful and frequent repetition by each student (of what he hears and reads) is an invaluable aid to memory.

Programmed instruction as a device for the church classroom will probably be used only minimally, largely because of the high cost of producing good programs. Also, it has its drawbacks, particularly with older pupils, in that it " controls " the students' responses. Pupils in the church, dealing with subject matter that calls for debate and questioning and personal reflection, are not helped to be more articulate about their faith when their thinking is held too strictly to a line determined by a programmer.

SYSTEMS APPROACH

We come now to another theory sometimes proposed for church classrooms — the " systems approach " to teaching. Not everyone who uses the expression can agree on which of the many definitions of the word " systems " is applicable to education. Some persons who know the history of systems in engineering and industry flatly reject the idea that the concept can be transferred to education.

Reduced to simplest terms, the systems approach, as employed by those who make and launch rockets and who are at home with giant computers, involves the isolation of all the factors that must be in operation to produce a given result. These factors are then introduced in a logical sequence; testing and retesting occur until the outcome is predictable. The rocket takes off when all systems are " go."

To apply a systems approach in the church's teaching, we would have to determine in advance a list of all the concepts we wanted a pupil to learn — from the Bible, the church's story, and theology. We would then have to arrange these in sequence. Then we would be required to set up conditions that would assure the introduction of the concepts at the proper time (some by pastors, some by teachers, others by parents, and so on). But nothing could be left to chance. The end product should be a student who had learned how to think theologically.

For perfectly obvious reasons, the systems idea in education, strictly interpreted, has little chance of wide acceptance in the church. Partly because the church, in its freedom, rejects controls and arbitrary means of doing things. Partly because the church has too little money to produce anything comparable to what we have described here. And mainly because everything in the church remains voluntary so far as pupils' participation is concerned. The church has no sanctions to apply; no pupil could be required to attend and to respond at each point in the sequence of instruction.

For better or for worse, this voluntary aspect in all church life is permanent. We may speak of "requirements" and of "certification" and other such legislative action to upgrade the quality of our teaching. But the mainstream of Protestant influence will retain the voluntary approach. This means that persuasive, deeply convicted leaders must work unceasingly to emphasize quality; they cannot expect their task to be made easier through some form of coercion on the part of denominational bodies.

IMPRESSIONS INTEGRATED

The teaching of concepts in the churches' classrooms, then, will be largely impressionistic. At every opportunity, teachers will be working with their pupils on single concepts, moving from one to another as Biblical material and churchly tradition dictate. In the final analysis, a fully integrated, foolproof curriculum for church study is neither possible nor desirable. We must trust a power greater than our own to carry on the integrative process in the pupil. Actually, this is what Christians mean when they speak of the " teaching of the Holy Spirit." It is the Spirit of God at work in a human heart when a pupil sees wholeness and unity to all the many ideas he has been considering over a period of time.

Such a way of thinking demands an integrative theological principle. For Christians, this is the Lordship of Jesus Christ, the living Word of God. Every idea, every concept, every fragment of thought, every bit of data — considered in a church classroom — point ultimately to what God has done in Christ. Our task as teachers is to help our students to grasp a clear but utterly mystifying truth — Jesus Christ himself. Nothing we do is simple; neither is it hopelessly complex. We are agents of God, working patiently and faithfully to magnify concept after concept. The many small impressions, grasped in no necessarily tight arrangement of sequence, can still be trusted to fall into shape and hold together, supplying a magnificent total impression — if we do our best with each one, always measuring our work against the full testimony of prophets and apostles. To grasp for the perfect teaching sequence is perhaps a natural inclination on the part of a curriculum planner. It may also be idolatrous, a striving after control over what remains in the domain of the divine Teacher alone.

NOTHING UNLEARNED

Although we can never succeed fully in doing so, we ought to make it our rule of thumb not to teach children anything they must unlearn later. The way must be left open for enlarged understandings of Biblical material. In many cases, this amounts to letting poetry be poetry and not trying to emasculate its profound truth by nailing it down to prosaic " facts."

For example, consider the Genesis story of the Creation. This story can still be taught to children in such a way that they grasp the essential truth — that God made everything and cleared the way for man to live trustfully upon the earth. Nothing can destroy God's providential care for his creatures. He is dependable, and we have our freedom because of his gift of life. Beneath and surrounding the story of Creation is the presence of Christ.

Allow young children to explore the text freely and to debate about it. They will readily dig out essential truth if the teacher keeps his heavy hand off their endeavor. The teacher's role is to listen, to underscore what is of lasting value, and to keep the way open for later discoveries. Young people who reject all religion because of Genesis are frequently the very ones who were taught in an arbitrary way; because they had to unlearn some of these carelessly church-taught " facts," their minds are not easily reopened to deeper meaning.

An infinite amount of misunderstanding could be avoided if teachers in the church could capture once and for all this need to keep doors open rather than to shut them tightly when children are young.

In all likelihood, this sort of arbitrary teaching, which produces flatness and too many square corners in the minds of children, has had something to do with the stereotyped images of theology commonly expressed even by noted intellectuals. We can find numerous examples in current literature of educational philosophers who speak of religion as a "closed system" in contrast to the exciting world of the physical and biological sciences, which, in their view, is a great "open system." They caution youth that faith is a vague word cloaking ignorance and the irrational. These exponents of rational values foresee a decline of theological endeavor and a brilliant, explosive future ushered in by the sciences.

A recent lecture by one such educator included the following list of rational values in the "scientific tradition":

1. Longing to know and to understand.
2. Questioning of all things.
3. Search for data and their meaning.
4. Demand for verification.
5. Respect for logic.
6. Consideration of premises.
7. Consideration of consequences.[10]

The clear implication was that these so-called rational values stemmed entirely from a modern, exciting scientific tradition that is multiplying human knowledge at an incredible rate. (A boy in school must, therefore, concentrate on learning how to think; it is hopeless for him to think he can master bodies of facts — they are obsolete before he graduates.) Equally clear was the implication that theology is a fixed body of traditional doctrine, closed and no longer capable of yielding new excitement and relevant ideas. Apparently the modern rationalist thinks theologians would have little interest in a list of seven rational values.

The dilemma presented by this type of popular thinking is acute. It is also very sad, for theology was the original science. It is progenitor to the rational values on that list! The church of Jesus Christ has undoubtedly fallen into error in times past, but there has never been a time when it was without men of vision who would willingly stake their lives for just such principles as these rational values represent. "Longing to know and to understand" and "consideration of consequences," and all the other values in between are characteristic of faithful servants of Jesus Christ. By no means are Christians the prisoners of a closed system; boldly they may claim to be true exponents of an open system, for they believe that truth in all its forms comes from God and sets men free.

Ironically, it remains for men of science rather than the educational philosopher to state a better case for unity in all human endeavor to know the truth. The great scientist of today (the man on the frontier, not the general practitioner necessarily) brings modesty and humility to his task. He sees no gain in setting faith *against* reason or in pitting science against theology and the arts. More and more, he speaks of unity within diversity, of a steady progress toward seeing wholeness in all things and all phenomena.[11] Even life and death are coming to be seen as somehow held together in a unity.

Have we gone too far afield? No.

We have ranged over very specific classroom problems, touching down on some philosophical considerations of overriding importance in our time. Few volunteer church school teachers today are helped to sense the enormous significance of what they are being asked to do. Others, realizing it quite fully, are struggling alone as though under a heavy burden.

Can the church as a whole afford to carry on business as usual in its educational efforts? The very future of our great hopes for church "renewal" rests in the hands of those who carry out the ministry of teaching. Unless they learn how to communicate concepts, how to face the exciting, joyous questions forever springing up around us, and how to think more expansively about ultimate aims and purposes, then we are all the poorer for the years to come. There was never a more urgent season for centering our thoughts on how to teach well.

CHAPTER 4

WEDGING IN SOME NEW IDEAS
(Hints on how to bring more data into sharper focus in the church classroom)

The teacher, after every class session, should ask himself two questions:

What did my pupils *see* during that hour we were together?

What did I ask my pupils to *do* today?

These questions are not related merely to inward vision or response. At this point they refer solely to activity in the classroom. A teacher should be able to list several things he asked his pupils to do, such as writing, reading an assigned passage, giving a report, acting out a scene, and countless other possibilities. Also, he should find it no problem to set down a listing of what the pupils saw: map, chart, poster, set of pictures, filmstrip, artifacts, chalkboard outlines, timelines, and many others.

In an average period of church instruction, carefully planned, a teacher might ask his pupils to do as many as four to six separate types of activity; and the pupils might have before them five to seven items to see.

But we do not have to go far to sit in on church school classes where pupils have been asked to do nothing but listen; furthermore, they have seen nothing but the teacher (and possibly the same pictures that have been hanging on the classroom wall throughout the year, and perhaps for years before that). They go home with no visual images other than the movements of the teacher and with only spoken words to recall.

Since it is a well-established fact that we remember only about a third of what we hear, in comparison to at least two thirds of what we see, what does this say about classroom practice in the church? We are not even beginning to employ as many devices for learning as we ought. If this is the case in our teaching of children and youth, it is doubly so in adult groups. We should greatly multiply our efficiency in the use of audio-visuals.

STRIDES IN A-V's

Fabulous advances have been made in recent years in the field of audio-visual instruction. Sometimes referred to as "technology" in education, this is the field that brings into classroom use a wide range of electrically operated devices, nearly all of which are capable of vastly augmenting a teacher's effectiveness. That learning is multiplied through the use of these gadgets is hardly open to question. Pupils benefit greatly from the inventions.

Why have decision makers not seen the value in a well-equipped *laboratory for learning?* Would they be willing to invest as much in devices for teaching as they will spend for food storage, cooking, and dishwashing? Churches in America are reluctant to do without well-equipped kitchens. Hundreds of dollars go into stoves, refrigerators, sinks, cupboards, and miscellaneous items required for a modest church kitchen.

The following comparison of costs is suggestive:

KITCHEN	LEARNING LABORATORY
Stove	Overhead projector and screen
Refrigerator	Tape recorder and listening center headsets for eight
Cabinets	Two 8mm. single concept projectors
Dishes and equipment	Complete set of permanent supplies for poster-making and artwork
Dishwasher	Two cameras

If a church has plans for a second kitchen, as many congregations do, then the money for that one could be spent instead for a complete closed-circuit television studio (now possible for $7,000 or so).

The reason that congregations have made so little imaginative use of all the possible pieces of equipment now available is actually twofold: most professional church educators are not audio-visually-oriented; the classroom teachers and other parish personnel lack information on all the things that are available.

All it would take to get a wave of interest started would be for just a few leading pastors to write and speak extensively about the excellent learning laboratories they personally had raised the money to equip, and in which they personally had shown continuing interest. Other churches would come to visit, and gradually the ideas would catch on. It would happen even faster if committees of influential laymen began to promote educational media with zeal.

What the church's professionals have not yet taken into full account is the impact of these media in general education today. The denominations are still principally pre-occupied with the techniques of yesterday, nearly all of which were tied to the printed page. We can no longer rely on the printed page alone *if* we are committed to up-dating and improving classroom practice. Too many other good ideas have come along. The other devices pose no threat whatever to editors and personnel whose gifts are in the literary field; in fact, films, recordings, and other visual materials require even greater editorial skill. They challenge the creativity of everyone at all interested in teaching.

Public education shares the same problems faced by the church in helping teachers to gain skills. Many school-teachers lack the problem-solving ability they need. A currently popular idea is to ask highly skilled master teachers to record good classroom practice on film and on video tape. As other teachers watch these model situations, they pick up new ideas for their own use, just as they would if they personally visited and observed classrooms in other schools.

In fact, audio-visuals are no longer spoken of as " aids " to teaching. Recognizing that films, television, and recordings actually *teach*, a newer, more descriptive term for them is " mediated teachers." [12] Any school now has before it three choices:

1. Classroom teachers alone.
2. Mediated and classroom teachers, in combination.
3. Mediated teachers alone.

The church, conceivably, might face similar choices as it made certain key curricular decisions. Certainly, the thinking about how to make wise use of mediated teachers ought to be occurring at the curriculum planning stage rather than solely at the classroom implementation stage.

If we were to conduct a survey of church decision makers throughout the country, asking them to state all they knew about the following items, we would find the percentage who could reply intelligently to be shockingly low:

1. Overhead projection.
2. Listening centers.
3. Single-concept 8mm. film.
4. Portable closed-circuit television.

Yet all these things have marvelous possibilities for use by the church in its teaching ministry. All are economically feasible on a cooperative basis. (See Chapter 7.)

Suppose we devote the next few pages to sketching out some ideas about just these four items:

1. *Overhead projection.* In early years, the projectors of this type were very large and clumsy. Today they are compact and portable, more efficient and easier to use. A lens on a standard focuses on specially prepared transparencies (usually about eight by ten inches in size).

The operator faces his pupils as he lays the transparency on the glass-topped base of the machine. He does not need to turn his head if he is sure of his transparency and the focus. The image on the surface below is nicely magnified on a screen behind him. If this is one of the new tilted, lenticular screens, there is no distortion and no need for darkening the room at all. (New projector models of all kinds, together with the greatly improved screens, have practically eliminated the darkening problem.)

As the transparency is projected, the teacher may mark on it with a grease pencil or with new liquid markers in a variety of colors. These are water-soluble and will wipe off easily so that the transparency may be used again. Also, the teacher may use any number of overlays; the only requirement is that these register accurately with the original.

In the preceding chapter, we alluded to Acts 6:1 as a Bible verse with a variety of concepts. One teacher took the passage Acts 6:1-7 as the basis for a special session on how to use Bible study resources. He chose to illustrate each type of resource with a transparency for the overhead projector.

First, he showed pages from *The Interpreter's Bible,* choosing the exegetical notes on this passage concerning the choice of seven deacons. The next transparency was from a theological wordbook which included an entry on deacons. The third was from a Bible dictionary which gave a definition of " daily distribution." Fourth and fifth were an atlas map showing Antioch (home of Nicolaus, the proselyte) and a page from a concordance indicating that Prochorus was mentioned nowhere else in the Scriptures. As each transparency was projected, he used the grease pencil for underlining and emphasizing words and phrases. He held up each book so that the class could see the sources from which the transparencies were taken. This procedure of taking a group through a careful study of a Bible passage with the aid of five types of study resources was what we might call " simulation." It was as if the pupils were looking over the shoulder of a serious Bible student at work. Once the exercise had ended, they were given copies of all the resources and asked to study other assigned Scripture passages on their own.

Only the overhead projector could make such a procedure so effective. The attention of the class members was fixed firmly on the magnified images; the members were led through the study systematically, getting the " feel " of doing research as it progressed.

Overhead projection is superbly suited to the presentation of time lines, map studies, and general outlines. The advantages over the chalkboard or the newsprint easel are obvious. Items may be viewed more easily and with greater speed. And probably because the visual impact is stronger, the projected images seem to be remembered longer.

2. *Listening centers.* Tape recordings are not new to anyone, but even these are seldom used in the church classroom. One of the reasons is that teachers do not think the pupils give full attention when all members of a class are required to listen simultaneously. They distract one another.

Good news, therefore, are the new listening centers that supply headsets for six or eight pupils, each headset plugged into the recorder; this makes it possible for rotating groups from the class to sit at a round table and give their undivided attention to the taped material. More elaborate centers supply individual carrels for pupils. At these there is nothing whatever to distract each listener.

Listening usually should have a purpose. The pupil should be supplied with pencil and paper or other materials. As he listens he either takes notes or acts upon oral instructions, or studies accompanying guides or texts.

Suppose that a teacher of sixth-graders is helping his pupils to reexamine the meaning of the Lord's Supper as it is celebrated in their church. He obtains an edited tape that includes excerpts from the liturgy employed in the service. Also, he has copies of the denominational service or prayer book at hand, as well as a collection of pictures showing the table, the elements, and scenes characteristic of the celebration. With the tape in the machine and all other items arranged neatly at a table for six to eight pupils, he asks that many members of the class to put on headsets. They listen, read, and inspect the pictures while the teacher and the other members of the class are at work in another part of the classroom. When the tape has ended, one of the pupils turns off the machine and the listeners rejoin the group. The teacher is prepared to quiz them when they return. Meanwhile another group of boys and girls can move to the listening center. The teacher has only to rewind the tape while they are adjusting their headsets.

The number of possibilities for such a listening center is almost endless. It is equally suitable for older pupils and young children.

No teaching staff should exclude the possibility of using the *telephone* in the classroom. New types of speaker phones can be installed inexpensively. Voices carry well within a range of seven feet, and additional amplifiers may be attached easily. Pupils may interview citizens in the community (such as older persons and shut-ins, many of whom have extraordinary talent and knowledge to share). Or they may tap the resources of distant personnel — noted personalities who would be willing to speak with the class briefly. Further, the telephone makes cultural exchanges possible when travel is either impossible to arrange or too costly.

3. *Single-concept 8mm. film.* For years teachers have complained that motion pictures, while dramatic and helpful in teaching, have presented logistical problems. They are not always available when desired, and it is difficult to show a brief segment of a film — a segment that may be

the only part germane to a subject under discussion. Also, the threading of the traditional projector requires skill on the teacher's part. Additionally, there is the problem of high costs for renting or purchasing 16mm. films.

The current trend is toward more and more use of relatively inexpensive 8mm. film. Gaining popularity are the small four-minute film loops mounted in plastic cartridges. These can be inserted into a tabletop projector instantly; they play and replay with no threading problems. Stocks of the cartridges may be kept in a desk drawer or special file.

Each four-minute loop treats a single concept. It can be used at a moment's notice at the appropriate point in a class discussion. Or it may be placed in a study carrel to which an individual student may be referred for study on his own. Or it may be used by a small group of students at a separate study table. Even a kindergarten child can operate the foolproof projectors that are used for this type of cartridge.

Possibilities for church use of 8mm. media are likewise innumerable.

In the Arizona Experiment in Biblical Studies and Teaching, a group of amateurs produced a four-minute loop entitled *How to Use a Bible Concordance*.

The color film opens with a concordance shown together with a Bible, between bookends. We then look over a teacher's shoulder as he examines the volume, finds a Bible citation in it, then turns to the Scriptures themselves to locate the passage and read for meaning.

A mimeographed guide was prepared to accompany this self-instructional film. The producers located a number of persons who had neither seen nor heard of a Bible concordance. Providing each with a copy of the guide, the film in a cartridge, and a table on which he could examine a concordance, they discovered that each person was able to make use of the book on his own after viewing the film. All those tested in this way reported that they felt the film actually taught them a useful piece of information in an efficient way.

One advantage to 8mm. material is that it can be produced by the teacher himself, in color, on a very small budget. Pupils can be enlisted to aid in the production by designing artwork, posing scenes, and handling technical details.

Producing a four-minute loop can require from ten to thirty hours of work. Once completed, it remains available for use on many occasions.

A concept should be chosen carefully, then the shooting scenes for the cameraman plotted on a storyboard. Each shot or sequence is described on a small index card, and these cards are inserted on a board that has rows of shallow pockets, permitting easy removal and rearranging of the cards. The storyboarding procedure is essential, for it helps to tighten the sequences and to eliminate repetitious or unnecessary shots.

The new type of camera with zoom attachment and reflex lens has taken the guesswork out of 8mm. motion photography. The rank amateur can produce good teaching sequences.

The single-concept film is usable for teaching skills and facts, but it is especially useful as a means of bringing cultural data into the classroom. (For example, archaeological finds could be viewed from all angles on 8mm. loops. With a pointer, an expert could indicate, in the film, what the pupils might tend to overlook.)

4. *Portable closed-circuit television.* It is now within range of possibility for churches to make use of portable equipment to produce their own video recordings. The tapes may be played back instantly over blank channels on any television set. Tapes, though fairly expensive to start with, may be used over and over, just as other recording tape.

The camera, video recorder, and monitor are in effect a portable closed-circuit studio.

The value of this type of equipment for improving teacher performance can be appreciated. A segment of good teaching, recorded and replayed for potential teachers, serves as an excellent model. The advantage over " live " demonstrations is in the fact that veiwers may witness the same scene numerous times, and demonstrations need not be repeated in so many locations. The machine may be stopped at any point so that observers can see, hear, then discuss at length.

In the classroom itself, a locally produced video recording can bring in persons and events from the community more frequently than would otherwise be possible (in the form of interviews, news reports, and documentaries). Pupils, too, can assess their own progress in role-playing, formal drama, music, and other activities as they are recorded and replayed for critical viewing and discussion.

Curricular revision by denominational agencies could be undertaken far more realistically if editors and writers could review on video tape a series of actual examples of what transpired with a given set of materials in a number of normal parish classrooms. Also, nationally produced segments of video material could be distributed for use on local equipment. Again, this thoroughly adaptable wonder of electronics is limited in its usefulness only by the creativity of teachers in the church who have the drive and vision to make use of them.

For many years now a much-neglected area of church curriculum development is the setting in which pupils are culturally deprived, or disadvantaged. This includes inner-city areas, remote rural regions, poverty-ridden communities, and ethnic groups such as Spanish-speaking or Indian Americans. Denominational planners continue to fret over how to adapt printed materials for use with these groups of special need. Actually, the problem is how to bring the best communicative skills and cultural materials into these settings. The answer is not necessarily something printed. All the electronic devices we have been discussing in this chapter are of inestimable worth in the situation where children and youth have not come to think of audio-visuals as commonplace.

In a New York experiment, young children from slum areas made their own 8mm. films with a grant of educational funds under a poverty program. In the Chicago City Church Project of the United Presbyterian Church, disadvantaged youth were caught up in earnest discussion of color slides of famous art, shown to the accompaniment of music familiar to them. This became an opening wedge for discussions on the meaning of life.[13]

What we are saying is simply that educational technology has made it possible to bring the happenings of the world — and the planets as well, in this space age — directly into the classroom. A much wider variety of stimuli to learning can be at the teacher's fingertips. There is little excuse for boredom anymore. And all these exhilarating developments cannot be ignored by the classroom teachers of Christian congregations. They will do so only to the impoverishment of their students. This is true for the church not only in this country but also throughout other nations. Think of the possibilities for improved communication among Christians engaged in world mission!

DREAMS AND REALITY

It can be a thoroughly shattering experience to compare dreams like these with the realities we face in countless church classrooms. So many of them reek of *neglect.* Lighting and ventilation are often poor, and color schemes may be ill-conceived.

We are all aware of how remnants tend to accumulate and to clutter storage space. Neatness and order are hard to maintain even under the best of circumstances, and the more so where facilities are inadequate for our supplies.

Money is lacking in most parishes for adequate chairs, tables, musical instruments, and other equipment. Children frequently sit on odd assortments of chairs, many of them at a poor height.

Of course, there is no excuse for a teacher to be untidy and uncaring about how his classroom is arranged. We may not be able to afford the best of equipment, but we can be clean and supply a businesslike work space for the pupils. That this, too, is so often lacking can be enough to drive the really concerned Christian educator out of his wits. But the greatest problem of all is the professional who shows a lack of concern about classroom arrangement.

Every beginning teacher in the church should make it an aim to bring something new into his classroom for the pupils to *see,* at every study session. This goes for the kindergarten "wonder table," but it also applies to every other class, including adult groups. Artists and persons of talent and accomplishment can be located in any community. Their services should be enlisted for creating educational exhibits such as dioramas, posters in three dimensions, and special bulletin boards. These items should never be left up longer than a week or two. When pupils understand that the church classroom is a neat, orderly place where they can expect to find stimulating ideas offered creatively, they will appreciate it, and the teacher will find himself rewarded with a new sense of accomplishment.

Parish decision makers and the pastor should be supplied with films showing the best of church classrooms, together with a printed checklist for use on an inspection tour of their own church facilities. Then, as a body, they ought to go into every nook and cranny, asking themselves: How can we improve on this? What goals for improvement can we meet within the next six months?

Let the tour be semiannual, and see to it that new goals are established each time. Let a churchwide interest campaign be initiated in order to enlist people of talent and means who will pitch in and help!

HONORS FOR ACHIEVEMENT

Most teachers who are given support and encouragement, who are honestly made to feel that others care about the quality of their work and will supply them with needed equipment, will quickly begin to take fresh pride in classroom appearance.

Each teacher should be given more incentives to devise useful classroom techniques — such as occasional special recognition and perhaps an accolade in local newspapers or bulletins, with complete descriptions of how the techniques came into being. Ideas such as the following deserve applause:

1. One teacher employed several colors of chalk in making an outline of key ideas under discussion, such as blue for main headings, red for subheads, white for parenthetical remarks; students found this helpful as they copied and talked over the jottings.

2. A kindergarten staff made rhythm drums from painted coffee tins, with the drumheads made of standard glued-on plastic lids. Felt decorations were added to the sides of the drums.

3. A teacher of seventh grade regularly made mimeographed copies of Scripture passages to be studied in class sessions, triple-spacing the typing. This enabled students to insert notes and captions, and to underline and encircle key words.

4. With a class of third-graders, a teacher supplied a large chart on which he had lettered several multiple-choice statements. To the left of the listed choices for each statement, he wrote " Yes " for the correct one, and " No " for the two incorrect ones. Masking tape was placed over each yes and each no. The students were asked to read the statements, consider which ending they would choose, and peel off the masking tape at the left to discover whether they had chosen correctly. Once the correct choice had been verified, the teacher used a red felt-nibbed pen to draw an arrow from the opening words of the statement down to the correct answer. This latter procedure helped to reinforce the correct response in the pupils' thinking.

5. A teacher of first and second grades clipped a number of pictures of persons from magazines, mounting them on posterboard without captions. He then distributed them to the pupils and asked them to use one or two words to describe the feeling or action they thought the pictures

suggested. A picture of a Buddhist monk from Vietnam produced the same response in more than half a group of fourteen pupils. They said, " He's thinking." From this exercise, the teacher led into the fact that the apostles had deep feelings as they tried to carry on the work given to them by Jesus. How, he asked, did Peter feel when he was put into prison? How did other Christians feel as they heard the news of his imprisonment? of his miraculous release?

6. Throughout a year of study on the church, a teacher of junior highs would include the singing of hymns either composed or sung in the different eras of Christian history. This would occur at any appropriate time in the class session, and the words would be discussed at the relevant moment. Such an integrated introduction of hymns seemed to be of greater value than the same choices sung in a formal period of worship.

7. A teacher of fifth-graders enabled his pupils to read the Bible with greater understanding by helping them to develop the habit of associating questions with each complete statement. He began by writing the current day, month, and year on the chalkboard and labeling it " A " for " Answer." Then he said, " The obvious ' Q ' (' Question') to go with this ' A ' is, ' What is today's date? ' " Next he wrote several facts, each a bit more abstract than the preceding one, and labeled them " A's." The pupils composed possible " Q's " to match with them. The teacher, satisfied that everyone understood this simple procedure, directed the pupils to a Bible passage and asked them to apply the same technique. With pencils and paper at hand, the boys and girls were soon converting sentences into questions. A test indicated significant improvement in their comprehension of Biblical material.

These ideas are by no means unique, but they are given as examples of the kind of creativity that is rare in church classroom practice. Creativity is not limited wholly by budget and equipment. A teacher with a will to be creative can do so with things as common as brown paper bags and paper clips. But he must *want* to, must think it matters, must care enough to plan in advance.

Who will see that new ideas are constantly being wedged in? That is a question every church must consider.

CHAPTER 5

AN HOUR IS REALLY QUITE A LONG TIME
(A second look at a lament, and an optimistic view of a limitation)

When any professional judgment gains wide acceptance and is no longer challenged, this is always a good time to ask: But is it really true? Has everything been taken into account? Progress in human thought and affairs depends on such second-looking — the questioning of conclusions, even those of the experts.

For years now, the judgment of professionals regarding weekly (Sunday) church school has been a lament voiced with regularity and verbatim consistency in literature and forums. The present writer is not excepted from those who have said unanimously:

"We haven't enough time. It is a hopeless business to try to teach well in forty to fifty hours a year, with those hours falling a week apart in the pupils' experience. We must have new schedules and larger blocks of time before we can make any gains in church teaching."

What about this profound, widespread sense of discouragement over scheduling and the time limitation in the typical church's educational ventures?

Two assumptions are implicit: that the more time a teacher has with his pupils, the better; that the closer together class sessions occur, the greater the chance that pupils will remember what they experience.

These largely undisputed assumptions have sparked serious disenchantment with Sunday school among professional Christian educators. They see no alternative except to campaign for ridding the church of a stereotyped pattern of Sunday morning teaching. In its place, the proposals usually offered are for weekday church classes or for released-time religious education (a term applying to the practice of allowing public school pupils to go to church-sponsored instruction during school hours).

Headlines such as " Church School Now Held on Tuesdays " have not been infrequent in recent years. In some communities the trend has definitely swung toward staggering the teaching schedule throughout the week. Teachers are frequently quoted as having been reluctant to try the idea, then having to revise their feelings. Many have found the tension of " getting through on time " greatly reduced. The church buildings can be utilized more efficiently, and pastors can be involved in the program, whereas their Sunday schedules militate against it.

Parents sometimes confess, negatively, that they like the weekday classes because they are then freed to leave town (and the church behind!) on weekends.

In some American communities, the movement to weekday instruction has a slim chance among church decision makers. Reasons are varied. Some parents in larger families rebel at the idea of chauffeuring their children to and from the church building as many as four or five times a week. Odd scheduling of public school hours may make consistent church scheduling during the week an exasperatingly complicated business, if not altogether impossible. Some teachers are employed full time and cannot get off work at the right hours. Many congregations have vociferous advocates of a "Sunday school is best" policy. Some pastors frankly worry over what to do, in limited facilities with limited staff, if there is an influx of children from neighboring congregations — attracted by the novelty of the schedule and taken away from the worthy class offerings in the Sunday programs of their own parishes.

This sort of movement and countermovement with respect to scheduling and the use of available time is undoubtedly a healthy sign. Creative patterns have emerged here and there, eliciting enthusiastic comment.

One simple factor, not at all insignificant, is the matter of *dress*. On Sundays in many congregations, pupils tend to wear their best clothes, and this formality lends a certain stiffness to the class period. (Curricular periodicals still include the warning to female teachers, "Don't wear your hat in the classroom.") When classes are held during the week, the atmosphere is more relaxed and pupils dress casually as they normally do in afterschool hours. Boys and girls feel less inhibited when it comes to classtime participation.

Another factor not previously mentioned is the experimental idea of a paid staff for weekday instruction. Advantages to paying teachers inhere largely in the fact that the employing church can require certain credentials and standards of job performance. Exponents of the paid staff idea believe it brings better quality into the classroom and impresses pupils and their families alike with the seriousness of the teaching enterprise.

By-products of the non-Sunday idea in church education have to be weighed on both the positive and negative sides. Firm advocates of weekday classes often use extravagant language in speaking or writing about the disadvantage of Sunday classes, and this arouses ire and resentment among those who have made heavy investments in traditional programs — investments of time, energy, and loyalty, not to say money. Supporters of Sunday school, on the other hand, lay themselves open to stereotype when they resist change and cite reasons for shunning innovation on the implicit grounds that untried approaches are of necessity suspect.

Two possibilities loom large: 1. We may be experiencing a kind of debate that can end only in a draw, with few issues really examined in an enlightening way. 2. We may see the debate resolved, with Sunday classes either winning or losing out, but still no earnest searching for deeper problems.

Already the signs of tension and unthinking debate have appeared. It began in the late fifties when a nationally circulated news magazine proclaimed one writer's conclusion that Sunday school was the week's "most wasted hour." This article, rather mild in comparison with more strident criticisms heard since, brought sober pronouncements of denial from the National Council of Churches' Division of Christian Education, meeting at just that time in Cincinnati. They pointed to the great effort then being expended in curricular reform, and hailed the noble efforts of Sunday school teachers throughout the land.

THE ROOT ISSUE

What happens over and over again is that the root issue lies unexamined. Also, the conclusions tacitly accepted by professionals have not been questioned with sufficient vigor. Sidetracked into preoccupation with Sunday vs. weekday arguments, and with a multitude of tedious details having to do with scheduling and deployment of teachers and pupils, the professionals and laymen alike have not asked the right questions.

The really important queries should be:

How much can you do with an hour?

How much does it matter (for good or ill) *that succeeding class hours are a week apart?*

Hardly anyone anywhere consents to lay down the extraneous matters and think instead about these primary issues.

Is it a foregone conclusion, no longer really open to question, that an hour is not long enough for a teacher and pupils to accomplish really worthwhile things? And can we conclude decisively that weekly class periods are a handicap to education?

If the answer to both questions is yes, it has not been spoken convincingly. Writers and speakers take a swift skip forward and plead for " more hours " (difficult to come by) on a schedule calling for greater frequency of meeting (possibly) or longer blocks of time for concentration (such as weekends). They pass over the fundamental matter of *what an hour can be worth.*

And those who speak of a solution to current problems through a process of rescheduling, are often so carried along by their enthusiasms that they obscure the underlying facts — not much time for actual teaching has been gained by the shifts, and the time between periods of study is still more than just a day or two. In their pleasure at having surmounted the Sunday-school-as-usual mentality, they forget that the very same questions still lie below the surface, not really pondered.

The fact that this happens repeatedly is not surprising. Nearly all theoretical questions continue to be discussed quite apart from empirical consideration of classroom data. It is far easier, on the surface of it, to decide that Sunday is the problem than it is to sit in on what happens Sunday with *other* questions in mind: What is right or wrong about the teaching and learning during this hour? Has maximum efficiency been attained?

To put it quite bluntly, doing away with Sunday school, and all the old images surrounding it, will *not* guarantee that pupils receive better teaching, or learn any more. Sunday in itself is not the problem, though we might wish it were. The problem is what to do with an hour, regardless of where it falls on the clock or the calendar. This is where the crisis really lies, as any frequent classroom visitor will affirm.

A Discrepancy

The discrepancy between the professionals' views and the views of the classroom teachers is very great. The trained educator, aware of all the possibilities for using class time, assumes widespread agreement among the laymen with his claim that an hour is inadequate for teaching-learning. He knows the enormity of the church's educational task because his vision has been enlarged through the years.

The volunteer classroom teacher, not versed in either content or technique, does not automatically sense that his hour is inadequate. He makes remarks like the following, and surely these indicate small appreciation for the preciousness of every minute:

"We don't always have enough material to fill the time, so we dismiss a little early."

"We need more 'activities' to fill the time after the 'lesson' has ended."

"But if we eliminated the twenty-minute service of worship, how would we use that extra time?"

" We can't 'hold their attention' more than a few minutes. A full hour would seem too long."

" It takes a lot of preparation to teach for an hour, and we're too busy to do anything additional during the week."

" We never start till most of them get here, and that's usually fifteen minutes late."

To repeat, it is plainly evident that the trained teacher uses time to greater advantage and is, therefore, sensitive to its swift passage. Also, he knows when time is being wasted and students are, consequently, being deprived of opportunities for learning. But he represents perhaps one teacher out of twenty.

The other nineteen teachers, chiefly through no fault of their own, lack the sensitivity to time's importance. They have no basis for realizing that a good part of every hour with their pupils is indeed *wasted*. It slips by, neither eagerly grasped nor efficiently used. More often than not, it is there to be " filled," from these volunteers' point of view. They think an hour is a long time.

The professionals and those persons with a modicum of training voice the lament on a lack of time. The other 95 percent of our teachers are not viscerally involved in this issue. When various alternatives to Sunday teaching are proposed, the whole matter is difficult for many laymen to debate. They have not experienced the same frenetic anxiety regarding a weekly hour of classroom time. To move the classes to a weekday seems, to them, to be only a matter of transferring the same patterns of working to some other time.

Wasted minutes can multiply on Thursday evening in quite the same way as on Sunday. Are the redeemed (efficiently employed) minutes of any greater benefit to teacher and pupil at one point in the week than at another?

The answer would appear to be that good, or poor, teaching is not fundamentally related to scheduling. The quality of teaching can be improved only by cutting through to the main issue — how to redeem fifty or sixty minutes so that, in the end, teachers can be said to have *taught* and pupils can be said to have *learned*.

LONGER THAN BEFORE

All factors considered, the lament about the shortness of an hour is probably without secure foundation. Sixty minutes is really quite a long time. It is longer now than it used to be. We have learned from radio and television — universally recognized examples — how memorable a wallop can be packed into thirty, or even fifteen, minutes. A full hour possesses overwhelming potential.

And what about the forty-hour year (or in some churches, the fifty-hour year)? That is a long, long time for teacher and pupils to be engaged in learning things. Considering the fact that a child may spend ten or twelve years in classes, all devoted to essentially the same subject matter — what God in Christ has done for them — we have fewer reasons for despair than we might think at first. If we used all this time well, we could accomplish much, much more than we are presently able to do. For today, fully a third to a half of every class hour in the typical church is wasted, pure and simple — either frittered away on fruitless motion or poorly planned and hence empty of value for the pupils.

From one vantage, it appears that professional Christian educators have seen a forest without focusing upon the trees. They becloud the church's teaching ministry by complaining of limitations and making the job seem complex beyond any possibility of our achieving any concrete goals. This need not be the case. Without risking oversimplification, we can surely say that it is *possible* to teach children the story of God's activity in Israel from Abraham until now. And it is possible to convey the dramatic meaning of God's reconciling entrance into humanity's plight through the life, death, resurrection, and ascension of Jesus Christ, his Son. Moreover, it is possible to explore again and again our own call to respond (in every walk and condition of our lives) to what God has done. None of this requires unlimited time.

The remainder of what we commonly teach in the church is subsidiary to the foregoing. Christ is at the center, and he is also at the beginning and the end. Where this reality embraces the teacher and claims *his* life, then he finds new power for helping to share its meaning with others.

Thousands of facts and ideas — many of them paradoxical, most of them challenging to the mind — enrich a Christian's life. The gospel of Christ is no commonplace, flat religious phenomenon; it is rich beyond all our capacity for study and thought. Even so, the formal teaching ministry of the church — so vitally necessary — need not seek a full explication of everything anyone *could* learn. That would be enough to lead even a scholar into despair. We are not asked to teach everything — we are to teach what must be known in order to witness a good confession of faith in Jesus Christ. The " system " is " open," but the essentials — *the ways of thinking and responding* — are teachable. Given an hour every week or so, and given a teacher who appreciates and uses it well, we can still do a very creditable job, whether it be on Sunday or any other day.

We need fresh, detailed evidence of what can happen in

an hour of teaching in the church, evidence like the following:

Six boys and girls entered the classroom approximately five minutes early. The teacher was ready for them. On a chalkboard he had lettered " Acts 6:8-15; 7:54-60," the passages to be studied that morning. He asked the pupils to find this account in the Bible and to copy any words that they did not understand; also, to copy and put a circle around words that they felt were the most important (" key words," he explained). Lined paper and sharp, new pencils were at hand. Chairs were neatly arranged at the work-study tables; Bibles were available there for those who had not brought their own.

As two other pupils arrived, just one minute before classtime, they were given the same assignment. By 9:33 A.M. three more pupils had entered. The teacher, having greeted everyone, faced these eleven boys and girls and conducted a review that went like this:

" The last time we were here, we talked about seven men who were chosen to be helpers in the church of New Testament days. What were these men called? "

Pause . . . silence.

A boy said, tentatively, " Deacons? "

" Yes! " The teacher put the word " deacons " on a wall chart, writing with felt-nibbed marker.

" And what did the deacons do? "

Two pupils answered:

" They helped serve tables."

" They helped the poor widows."

TEACHER: Do you remember any of their names?

GIRL: Was Stephen one of them?

TEACHER: Yes. And it's about Stephen that we are to read today. (Time: 9:35.)

TEACHER: Let us pray, asking for God's help in our class today. (Teacher offered free prayer.)

Six latecomers entered the room after the prayer. The teacher nodded them to seats. He then told the story of Stephen in his own words, illustrating with two pictures from an art file. He pointed out details in each picture, carefully reminding the pupils: "No one really knows how anyone in the Bible looked. This is the way two artists have pictured Stephen." (Teacher moved around from group to group; pupils now occupied seats at three tables.)

TEACHER: Now those who came early were reading Stephen's story from the Bible. Where do we find it?

One pupil gave a page number from his Bible. At teacher's prompting, he read the book, chapter, verses, cited on the chalkboard. (Time: 9:43.)

TEACHER: Let's all find this story in our Bibles. You follow as I read it aloud. (Brief instruction supplied on the location of The Acts.)

The teacher read the passage aloud, stopping to use a map of Jerusalem in New Testament times, and also to explain key words and those difficult to understand (grace, wonders, signs, synagogue of the Freedmen, Spirit, instigated, blasphemous, scribes, council, etc.). He put some of these words on the wall chart. Also, he interpolated that ch. 7:1-53 contained Stephen's sermon. He suggested the sermon's content. (Time: 9:49.)

At this point, the teacher selected a boy to play the part of Stephen and explained that he and the group would pantomime the story while the teacher gave the narrative from a special script he had prepared. The "stage" was set, Stephen took his place, and three scenes were enacted: Stephen before the council, Stephen preaching, and Stephen being stoned to death by the angry mob. (Another boy played the part of Saul, standing by.) (Time: 9:56.)

When everyone was seated again, the teacher brought out two cards on which he had lettered in red the words "persecution" and "martyr." Through simple explanations like the following, he helped to give meaning to the words:

"Hurting someone because of what he believes or stands for is persecuting him. Persecution is this kind of being hurt. Sometimes persecution means killing or injuring others. Sometimes it means hurting people's feelings very deeply over and over again.

"A martyr is a person who dies or endures persecution. But a deeper meaning for the word 'martyr' is 'a person who is willing to go through anything because of his belief and faith.'

"We speak of Stephen as the first Christian martyr. He and many other Christians were persecuted. Does anyone ever become a martyr today? And is there persecution now?"

With a few slight leads from the teacher, the boys and girls began to volunteer examples of persecution in race relations in America and of political persecution in Vietnam and other parts of the world.

TEACHER: What does the story of Stephen tell us about being persecuted?

BOY: That you'll die.

TEACHER: Yes, Stephen did die. But maybe I haven't asked the question in the right way. What difference does it make whether we stay faithful the way Stephen did?

GIRL: God cares, and he wants people to be full of courage like Stephen.

TEACHER: And what about today? Christians sometimes suffer because they try to bring a better life to people of all colors and races. How do you think God feels about them?

BOY: I think God cares. But why is it that some people get hurt and others don't? (All pupils very thoughtful.)

TEACHER (slowly): I really don't know why. And no one does. But God understands. He is with us all when we try to be true to what we believe.

There was a slight restlessness among the pupils. They had thought deeply and now needed a change of pace. The teacher sensed this and brought discussion to a close by suggesting that the group move over around the piano. He took his seat on the bench and pointed to words of a hymn on a song chart at the side: " The People of the Way." He suggested that they sing, thinking about all the martyrs through hundreds of years, including today.

(At the end of the singing, even with pauses for improving the pupils' musical expression, the clock hands now stood at 10:07.)

The pupils went back to the worktables, and the teacher distributed drawing paper and drawing pencils. He also showed them lists of possible drawings and asked each one to choose what he would like to try drawing:

1. Stephen preaching.
2. Some men arguing with him.
3. A group whispering and plotting against him.
4. Stephen seized.
5. Stephen before the council.
6. Stephen stoned.
7. Stephen lying dead.

When choices had been determined, the pupils were put to work. The teacher moved around, giving encouragement to individuals. At 10:22, he gave a warning, "Just two more minutes." By 10:26, supplies were put away and drawings were ready to share. With a plastic substance, the teacher mounted one drawing of each scene on a wall, noting that the drawings would remain there until the class met again. The pupils were then asked: "What are the main things we've learned today? You tell me, while I make notes here on the chalkboard."

PUPILS: About Stephen. Martyrs. Persecution. Doing what we believe in. The church. We're people who belong to Jesus. Some people suffer more than others do.

TEACHER: You've suggested seven things we talked about — things we may have learned. Next time we meet, we'll be learning more about Saul, the man who stood by while Stephen was stoned. Before we go home, let us pray. (Teacher used liturgical prayer of thanks for saints and martyrs. Pupils left room at 10:30.)

What the pupils had *seen* during this session: Reproductions of two paintings by artists; chalkboard; wall chart; words on placards; song chart; their own drawings.

What the pupils had *done:* Research (by some); reading; discussion; acting out a scene; singing; drawing.

To be sure, there is nothing especially innovative about this third-grade class session. But it is extraordinary, as church classes go, for no time was wasted. The teaching began the moment the first pupils arrived. The atmosphere was businesslike, and the room was efficiently arranged. No outside interruptions occurred. Concepts were pursued in logical order. Pupils appeared to see a connection between the Biblical material and current events. Review in the succeeding session should be sufficient to help the pupils to place Stephen in their thinking as "first Christian martyr." The teacher's technique was primarily inductive. He began with Stephen's story and gradually led into the main point for discussion — the fact that men are persecuted and become martyrs because of what they believe and stand for. (He might have chosen to do it the other way around, taking the deductive approach by starting right off with the definitions of martyr and persecution, then letting Stephen's story follow as an illustration.)

Many themes were left unexplored. The sermon of Stephen highlights contrasts between the Christians and the religious parties of the Jews. All this material will have to be learned later by the boys and girls. But the way is open for this. Nothing was pushed upon them. Nothing was beyond their comprehension. Nothing would have to be unlearned.

What happened in this class might have taken place on a weekday afternoon rather than a Sunday morning. But that is a completely extraneous matter. The important thing is that it took only an hour, probably should not have lasted any longer than that, and was an efficiently conducted period in which some possibilities of learning were present. In forty to fifty such hours together a group of third-graders could get a very solid set of understandings about New Testament history. How well it all fitted together for them would depend on the teacher's ability to keep the boys and girls involved in repeated review of what they had learned.

Here is an outline of a *fifteen-minute segment* from a teacher's classroom diary:

A SEVENTH-GRADE CLASS

The subject under discussion was " parable." The fifteen pupils had just examined the fact that the New Testament describes Jesus' teaching as parabolic.

TEACHER: What is the root meaning of this word " parable "?

PUPIL: A parable is a story.

TEACHER: But is that enough to say? All stories aren't parables. What makes a parable different?

Silence . . .

Teacher wrote two words on the chalkboard in this way:

PARABLE

COMPARE

Then he underlined the " par " in each, and boxed that syllable:

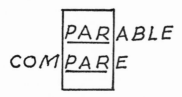

TEACHER: " Perhaps seeing these words in this way will help us to remember the chief characteristic of a parable. It is a story or an account of some familiar experience which is used to point to some larger, similar truth about God and his Kingdom. Jesus makes comparisons which are sometimes quite clear; at other times, the disciples do not understand."

The pupils were asked to turn to Luke, ch. 15. When they had found it in their Bibles, he said: "This chapter contains three parables of Jesus. Let's divide ourselves into teams, with three persons on each team. I want you to read the three parables and prepare to discuss later *why* you think Jesus told them. What was he *comparing?*"

(In less than two minutes, after some requests for clarification on the part of two teams, the pupils were at work — reading and making notes. The teacher moved from team to team, "hovering" over them and, by his attitude, urging total involvement in this project. The teams appeared to be finished within seven minutes.)

TEACHER: Now tell me what you found. What was Jesus' reason for telling these parables?

PUPIL: He was comparing lost sheep and lost people.

ANOTHER: And lost coins.

ANOTHER: The last one is the prodigal son. The son is like a sinner.

TEACHER: Yes, but *why?* What is the *reason* for these parables? There is a point of comparison you haven't told me about. Did any of you see something that ties all three parables together? If so, what is it?

Pause . . . restlessness.

PUPIL: Well, the word "lost" is in all three. Is that what you mean?

TEACHER: That's a good observation. These are parables of the lost sheep, the lost coin, and a lost son. But you still haven't mentioned something very important. R——, read aloud vs. 1-2, please.

R—— read as requested.

TEACHER: The next verse begins with what word?

Pupil: So!

Teacher: What does that suggest to you?

Pupil: Maybe Jesus was telling all these parables to get back at these scribes and Pharisees.

Teacher: Now you're getting to the point.

(Thirteen minutes had now elapsed. The teacher used the next two minutes, with questions and chalkboard jottings, to stress the unity of the three parables as a reply to Jesus' critics. God cares about sinful, separated men, and Jesus' own ministry must be compared to the special attention a shepherd gives to the lost sheep, a woman to a lost coin, a father to his lost son. The purpose of these parables is to defend and further to define the mission of Jesus.)

This fifteen-minute segment was followed by a highly pertinent discussion of the church's mission in the world of today. The pupils began to sense that the church cannot retreat to the safety of its own four walls. Its people must reach out in ministry just as Jesus himself did. The pupils were able to see meaning in the parables — meaning related to the church as they knew it.

There is no guarantee that all fifteen boys and girls developed an equal degree of awareness during this period of teaching, but something had been started, a foundation stone laid. An efficient use of a few minutes had helped to impress at least two elementary items upon the pupils' minds: " Parable " involves comparing a set of familiar circumstances with a God-man relationship; we have to look closely in the Bible to discover why a parable was used.

This sort of foundation was laid by a teacher who asked questions in logical order, who involved pupils in research, and who provided images in chalk to accompany his own brief presentations. The pupils would likely remember, at the subsequent class session, both what they had done as teams and what they had seen on the chalkboard.

(Incidentally, the teacher avoided using paintings that depicted the lost sheep, the lost coin, and the prodigal son. Instead, he searched for an artist's conception of Jesus confronting his critics, the Pharisees and scribes.)

Pupils taught in this way have gained something on which to build. Nothing has to be discarded from this sequence. For years to come they will be reexamining the church's ministry to the world, comparing it with Jesus' own ministry. The three parables of Luke, ch. 15, will be seen in the correct light, and not merely as three separate "Sunday school stories."

Here, however, we must observe once again that it took only a few minutes. Future segments of teaching should review and reinforce repeatedly what this teacher began with these seventh-graders. But no more time was needed, at this point in the pupils' experience, to lay the initial groundwork.

ADVANTAGE?

Just possibly, the span of a week between study periods in the church could prove to be an advantage. We tend to remember what stands out as an *occasion*.

One of the characteristics of our time is a steady onslaught of images, sounds, and other stimuli. It is difficult, even at the end of a single day, to recall in order what we have experienced. So many thoughts, so many choices, have been faced through the hours that we find it hard to reconstruct what we may have learned or sensed. For this very reason, a special period of instruction that occurs weekly may stand out as " special " in the pupils' minds.

College and graduate students would attest from experience that weekly seminars are sometimes recalled more vividly than the lecture courses that meet daily during a semester. Why? Because the seminar period stands out as an occasion to be remembered; it is not merely blended in with the students' everyday routine and thus obscured or blocked off from specific mental review.

To repeat once more, we ought not to echo unthinkingly the complaint that the church cannot accomplish much on a weekly calendar, in one-hour sessions. If each teaching session in the church is carefully planned, the pupils may begin to look forward to it as a unique undertaking. Far from hindering their progress, the weekly schedule may be an aid to their remembering.

The fact is that an hour is still a long time — perhaps longer than ever before now that we know better ways of filling it with stimuli to learning. And when a bright hour stands alone to be recalled for a week, it may be that this is more of an advantage than a handicap.

What counts supremely is our ability to do well with the teaching time we have. We cannot afford to waste those minutes which we may come to regard as precious.

CHAPTER 6

ADVICE: TEACH YOURSELF!

(Reflections on how a self-starting volunteer teacher can mature in his job)

The volunteer teacher in the church frequently protests: "But I'm a busy person! I don't have days to spend in study, and that's why I need simple helps I can use in a hurry."

The professional church educator tends to shrug off this protest. He meets it by saying: "But you must find more time, realizing how important your job is. You can't expect your work to be simplified for you." The teacher accepts this at face value; if he is conscientious, he develops a keen sense of guilt. But the situation with respect to his teaching remains the same — he admits he is forced by his busy schedule to postpone things till the last minute, and he limps along as best he can.

Is there a way to help the volunteer to do a better job without discouraging him with overwhelming assignments which he regards as hopelessly impractical? And without compounding his problems of personal guilt?

What he needs is a program of advice centered on: (1) how to utilize to the best advantage the preparation time that he has available and (2) how to cultivate a mind-set for each period he is to spend with his class.

The first step is learning to get the gist of prepared curricular materials — how to sift through the words to get the main ideas in mind. This can be done by noting printed headings and by underlining topical sentences in the paragraphs. If the class meets on Sunday (for instance only), the teacher should spend twenty to thirty minutes making a basic outline of the curricular material on the evening of the *preceding* Sunday or Monday. This is extremely important advice. His outline might look something like this:

1. Main ideas to be examined in class next week: (These are listed in logical order.)

2. Bible passages to be studied: (Citations listed.)

3. Techniques for classroom use: (These are listed — such devices as small-group discussion, research projects, tests, etc.)

This bit of work forms the groundwork for the teacher's week. Only if there are special materials to be prepared, gathered, or ordered, does the teacher need to refer again to the printed materials. He can now work from his own rough outline. As one teacher put it, " The lesson goes on the back of the stove to simmer for several days."

Throughout the week, the teacher should hold in his mind a mental listing of key concepts to be examined with his pupils. This mental listing serves as a kind of magnet, gathering to itself many small pieces of related information and data. All these become grist for the mill when last-minute study and preparation are undertaken.

As the teacher reads his daily newspaper, watches television broadcasts, talks with friends and neighbors, reads magazines and books, and spends time in personal reflection and prayer, he keeps his mental list in mind. Surprisingly often, he hears and sees things that prompt him to say to himself, " That will be important to clip out and share with my pupils," or " I mustn't forget to ask the boys and girls to consider that! " By Saturday, he is ready to spend a good hour — or possibly ninety minutes — thinking through a whole week's collection of pertinent ideas. (For example, pupils and teachers who have examined the issues of church-state relations in the twentieth century would find almost daily news items which should be considered along with prepared curricular materials.)

The teacher should plan also to spend at least part of an hour going over, repeatedly, any Bible passage to be studied in class. A good one-volume commentary and other Bible study resources should be consulted as needed. (Every professional church educator would be well advised to make certain that teachers know how to make best use of such resources. This can be done in a two-hour session; resources should include commentaries, dictionaries, atlases, concordances, and wordbooks.)

The final step in preparing for a class session is making a simple schedule to suggest how every minute of the hour is to be utilized. This outline will seldom if ever be used exactly as written. The experienced teacher will testify, however, that it contributes greatly to his confidence as he works in the classroom. A typical outline might begin as shown at the bottom of the opposite page.

If a teacher will work consistently in this way (the first half hour's labor a week ahead of time, the other two and a half hours close to the actual meeting time), he will be able gradually to acquire considerable skill in his job.

SIMPLE GOALS

Meanwhile, the teacher should set for himself certain minimum goals for continuing self-improvement:

1. *Acquiring a time line.* In any good Bible atlas one may find a chronological listing of dates assigned by scholars to the Biblical events from Abraham to apostolic times. These dates, placed on either a vertical or horizontal line, can be a great help to the teacher. All the books of the Bible, and the events they recount, can be placed on this time line. Remembering the exact dating is of no great importance; what matters is the general picture of relative time spans between major events and of relationships among the books of Old and New Testaments.

The same kind of device can be constructed for keeping principal happenings of church history in a clear sequence for memory. A number of simplified church history texts supply a listing of events in chronological order.[14]

When a teacher makes personal time lines of this sort, they are a valuable aid to memorizing the essential structure of Christians' Biblical and churchly heritage. One volunteer teacher of senior high school pupils, faced for the first time with a unit of study on Galatians, found that the text of this New Testament letter made no sense without

TIME	MAIN IDEAS	MATERIALS
9:30–9:35	Review of last session and introduction of today's theme	Chart from previous class meeting
9:35–9:45	Small-group study of Bible passage	Bibles, pencils, and paper
9:45–9:50	Reports from groups	Chalkboard for summary
Etc.	Etc.	Etc.

some background study of Abraham and patriarchal history. Lacking knowledge of the Old Testament, she had to do considerable research. This venture led her to see the importance of getting fixed in mind a Biblical time line. Now her Bible study is easier, and she doesn't have to wonder, each time she takes up the Scriptures, just how a given event relates to what has gone before or comes afterward. Her mental image of the time line helps her to "place" names, places, and happenings as she reads.

A few minutes given to reviewing time lines periodically can contribute steadily to a teacher's competence in the church's subject matter.

2. *Mastering classroom techniques.* A second area for continual review by the teacher is a fundamental list of teaching techniques suitable to the age group with whom he is working. This can be obtained from curricular publications and from research in age group manuals prepared by the various denominations.[15]

Having always in mind a collection of workable techniques is like having good recipes committed to heart or a good musical repertoire. The techniques can be employed when they will best serve the teacher's purpose. He need not be self-conscious in his choices; he simply selects what is best for communicating a given idea to pupils or for involving them in making essential discoveries. Techniques and content for an hour of instruction go hand in hand. Curricular materials offer in printed form the suggestions of editors and writers whose own teaching experience suggests certain ways of working in the classroom. These are not necessarily the best in every situation. But until a teacher has surveyed the field of possibilities and has begun to understand *why* the writers choose as they do, then he really does not have the freedom to rearrange and manipulate the material ("adapting it to his own needs," as the experts are prone to put it).

3. *Considering pupils' characteristics.* Knowing what the pupils are like in their general makeup, psychologically and physically, is an essential for a teacher. So reads every teacher manual ever produced. The problem seems to be that a few teachers work too hard at it, and most do not work hard enough.

Here is a teacher who is all wrapped up in technical language descriptive of what she thinks is the real condition of her pupils: "They are engaging in compensatory behavior," she says, "and this is a normal developmental stage for this age grouping."

What does she mean? She means that her class members have been acting up lately, and she thinks it is perfectly natural because children that age have a tendency to act one way in order to cover up how they feel or, perhaps, what they do not know.

But is her analysis accurate? Perhaps the kids are bored stiff by a dull lesson. Some other cause, more serious, may be at the bottom of the trouble. For this teacher, though, a little knowledge of psychological terms may have caused her to think too narrowly. In short, she may have been prevented from better relations with her pupils through too much superficial study of a highly technical field.

On the other hand, here is a teacher who, when faced by recalcitrance among pupils, may shrug the whole thing off: "That's kids for you! You can't do a thing with them!" He appears to lack a sympathetic inclination to learn what motivates the boys and girls.

In all likelihood, reading may not be the best way to

glean insight into the growth and development of children. Quiet, reflective observation of their behavior, coupled with a few conversations with good guidance counselors, school psychologists, and other *trained* observers, is probably a better way. Then what one reads can be dealt with in better perspective.

A teacher owes it to himself to become acquainted in an elementary way with some of the well-established data regarding human development. But he does well to avoid both perils — accepting the hasty conclusions of superficial study or discounting too readily the valuable insights experts offer into human behavior.

The foregoing are intended as hints on general areas of awareness that the teacher should cultivate. He can do this on his own. The more he gains in each area, the greater freedom he has for operating in the classroom.

No volunteer can learn everything all at once, nor should he feel that he must try to grasp beyond his immediate reach. The important thing is to accumulate both experience and understanding through steadiness in one's daily thinking and weekly preparation. Openness to new ideas is one of the most desirable traits in a teacher.

FREE TO LISTEN

The greater the teacher's personal competence, the stronger the likelihood that he will be a good listener, open to what others are saying. Having his subject matter and his teaching techniques well in mind, he no longer needs to be preoccupied with these at the expense of seeing and hearing. He is free to listen, free to know his pupils. One need not visit many class sessions before he is keenly impressed by a teacher's need to discover and enjoy that kind of freedom.

A teacher of four-year-olds, busily trying to follow her plans for the morning, was seeing the pupils off at the door, giving out their artwork to be taken home. She said, almost automatically, "David, take this home to your mother." He replied: "I can't. She has gone to be with God." Still not thinking, she responded: "Take it to her, David." He shouted: "How can I? She is with God!" He meant, of course, that his mother was dead. The teacher seemed never to catch the point. And why had she not known about David's mother? The class was not a large one; there had been time for her to learn about the homes of each of the boys and girls, but she had not grasped the opportunity.

The practice of distributing tags to children as they enter the room is sometimes offered as a way of helping teachers to learn the pupils' names. Instead, it often becomes a crutch; teachers rely on the tags and fail to work at connecting names with living persons. In one small congregation, teachers used name tags for fifteen or twenty pupils of the fifth and sixth grades through a year of class meetings. Their explanation seemed hardly credible: "We do it because more than half the children are Indians, and they all look just alike!" (Indians definitely do not look alike, any more than persons of other races do. These teachers were simply preoccupied by other things, lacking freedom to concentrate on name-learning.)

A number of good volunteer teachers hold strongly to the view that it is necessary to their work for them to set aside times when pupils can be invited to their homes for informal times just to help everyone get acquainted. Hearing this, one teacher of little experience responded: "Why, I wouldn't think of bringing boys and girls into my house. They'd wreck it." This reaction was not at all unusual. Perhaps it is typically symptomatic of our age. An air of detachment, a policy of noninvolvement, seems evident in so many human relationships today. Where the church's teachers, too, are slow to be outgoing and concerned about their pupils, we can be sure that children and youth will sense the fact. When all is said and done, the kind of human being a teacher is will determine to a large extent how the pupils react to his teaching.

To summarize, the teacher can do much to increase his competence by determining to *teach himself: what* the church has to communicate to people; *how* communicating can occur effectively so that pupils begin to hear and to respond; and *who* the pupils are — what they are like, how they react, and all the possible reasons why. In teaching, he must be himself, hoping the pupils may see in him a commitment to Christ as Lord, but knowing that he dare not offer himself as example. He can only pray that together he and his pupils will be confronted by those truths which the Holy Spirit alone can make effectual in their lives.

THOUGHTS WHILE TEACHING

The following is an account of a brief period that one master teacher spent with a class of third-grade children. The italicized material in parentheses is intended to reflect the teacher's mental processes as the period progressed.

TEACHER: Today we're going to pretend that we have a visitor who has never seen a Bible. He doesn't know anything at all about it, and we have to try to help him understand what it is.

PUPIL 1: Where is this visitor from?

TEACHER: (*The visitor could be from anywhere. I'll see where* they *think he might live.*) That's a good question. Where would *you* say he's from?

PUPILS: Africa? South America? North Dakota? Europe?

TEACHER: (*They've mentioned faraway places only. I'll point this out and ask why.*) You've given a lot of places. They're all pretty far away. Why so far?

PUPIL 2: Well, I'd say because people around here all have Bibles. It would have to be someone from some country where people don't go to church.

TEACHER: But people do go to churches in Africa, South America, and the other places you mentioned. You're right that there might not be as many Bibles in some parts of the world as in our own part of it. But still, the visitor could be from almost anywhere. There are people in our very own town who probably know almost nothing about the Bible. Let's go on now and see what you think we'd have to do about this visitor. What would we say or do first?

PUPIL 3: Let's give him a Bible, one like mine.

TEACHER: (*He prefers his kind of Bible. I'll ask why.*) Why do you say one like yours? Is it better than others?

PUPIL 3: My mother says mine is easier to read than the kind she and Grandmother have. It's . . . well, I guess it's more up-to-date.

TEACHER: (*I'll have to pause now and deal with this matter of translations. Better use the chalkboard.*) Most of you have the kind of Bible P—— is speaking about. It is a newer English Bible than the one G—— brought today. (*I am holding up both.*) G——'s is a King James Bible, translated into English and published first in 1611, more than three hundred fifty years ago. P——'s is a Revised Standard Version, a translation first published in 1952, not too many years ago. The Revised Standard Version is written in the kind of English we use today. The King James Version uses the language people spoke in England long ago.

PUPIL 4: You mean people said things like "Thou" all the time?

TEACHER: That's right, S———. "Thou" for *you* and "thine" for *yours,* and many other very old ways of saying things. We can still understand this way of speaking, but we don't use it anymore in our everyday speech. (*Write "King James Version, 1611," and "Revised Standard Version, 1952," on the chalkboard.*)

Pause.

TEACHER: Now, where were we? We'd just decided to give our visitor a Bible like P———'s. Then what would we do?

PUPIL 6: He'd say, "What's that?" (*Pupils are laughing.*)

TEACHER: Then what?

PUPIL 1: We'd say, "This is a Bible." (*They're laughing again, and it is a little amusing. I need to take another approach.*)

TEACHER: Now suppose I pretend to be the visitor. You've just said to me, "This is a Bible." And so I'm going to answer. I say: "It says 'Holy Bible' on the cover. What's this book about? What does 'Holy Bible' mean? Can you tell me?"

Pause. (*They're getting a bit restless. Third-graders aren't quite ready for too much of this type of role-playing. Will drop it altogether. Chalkboard probably best as next step.*)

Teacher writes on chalkboard:

βίβλος – book

Pupils perk up, startled by the strange characters.

TEACHER: (*They're interested in this. Will explain for a while.*) This is one Greek word for " book," written in the Greek language. It is pronounced bĭb'lŏs. Now watch as I write our own word " Bible " underneath:

βίβλος
Bible

See how the words do look something alike? (*I'll draw arrows for emphasis.*)

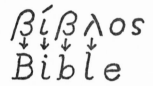

βίβλος
↓ ↓ ↓ ↓
Bible

PUPIL 5: That doesn't look alike to me. How do you get Bible out of those crazy letters?

TEACHER: (*This is the way C—— often reacts. His teacher at public school has told me about his problem in reading, and I know his parents are worried about it. He is really asking for help, in a sense, but I can't take a lot of time with it. Still, I won't ignore his problem either. The other pupils seem to understand.*) C——, look more closely, please. This Greek letter β is called beta — it looks like our *B*, doesn't it? Then comes a Greek letter called iota. It looks like a small *i*, doesn't it? Then here is another beta, or *b*. I agree with you that the next letter in Greek —

it's called lambda — doesn't look too much like an *l*, but in a way it does if we use our imagination. So, with that many letters — four, just so nearly alike, we can see how our word " Bible " is really from the very old Greek word that means book. The Bible is a *Holy Book* . . . but what does " holy " mean? That's the next question. Does anyone know what it means to call something holy?

PUPIL 4 (very hesitantly): Does " holy " mean . . . like . . . in church?

TEACHER: (*She has grasped the idea that a reverential feeling — in church, for instance — is something unique. She is a very sensitive child. She thinks this may have some connection with " holy," and this is partly right. I must encourage her; I'll accept her answer and build on it.*) Yes, S——, you have begun to get the idea. " In church " is something special or different from being in other places. The Bible, too, is special and different. Holy means *separated*, or we might say " separate from." The Bible is a book separate from all other books. What do you think makes the Bible holy?

PUPIL 1: Because it's about God?

PUPIL 3: It tells us about Jesus.

PUPIL 7: We can find out in the Bible how to live.

TEACHER: (*That last answer comes from B——. His father is a good friend of mine, and I've heard him talk about the Bible as a rule book. B—— may have caught something of this. If it comes up again, I may need to work on it. Better accept all these responses at this point.*) You have the general idea. We could tell an imaginary visitor that the Bible is special, different, because it is made that way by God himself. He is in the Bible, and when we read it we learn what he is like, what he has done in sending Jesus, and what he wants us to do. Would it be enough just to tell this much to a visitor? Would we need to say anything else?

PUPIL 2: We might tell him it's hard to understand. (More laughs.)

TEACHER: (*This is T——'s sense of humor coming through. He's right, though. Let's make something of this.*) You're right, T——. It isn't always easy to understand the Bible, even after we've worked hard at reading it. But we can understand much of it with a little help from teachers and others who have read the Bible carefully.

Let's all pick up our Bibles and turn to the first part called the Old Testament. (*I'm going to drop the " visitor" idea. It's served its purpose. They're all thinking about the Bible. We won't refer to the visitor again unless someone brings him up.*)

PUPIL 3: Hey! What does Testament mean?

TEACHER: A good question, P——. Testament is an important word. The Bible has two Testaments, the Old and the New. Testament is the same word as *covenant*.

PUPIL 3: I remember covenant. We talked about that. It's a *promise!*

TEACHER: (*I didn't really expect anyone to remember. But we did talk about covenant several weeks ago.*) P—— is on the right track. A covenant is a kind of agreement or contract in which someone makes a promise. When God makes a promise to men, we say he has made a covenant. The Old Testament is an old promise of God, and the New Testament is a new promise. (*Will stick to the simple motif of promise; they can learn more about covenant later.*) P——, you are the one who remembered when we used the word " covenant." What did God promise? And who heard him?

PUPIL 3: It was Abraham. But I don't know the rest.

TEACHER: God promised Abraham that he would make his family into a special people, and he wanted them to share what they knew about God with all others in the world. The Old Testament tells us about Abraham and all the people who came from his family. (*I'll draw a line on the chalkboard and put Abraham at the left.*)

Abraham _____

The Old Testament has much more in it than just about Abraham. God made his promise over again to another great man. Who would that be? Have you heard of another who received God's promise?

PUPIL 4: We talked about Moses.

TEACHER: (*Again, their memory surprises me. They show some signs of restlessness, though. I'll add Moses quickly, then change my approach just a bit.*)

Teacher returns to chalkboard:

Abraham, Moses _____

Yes, God made his promise to Moses. The Old Testament contains the laws that Moses gave to God's people.

Now I want to show you something I borrowed from the library. This is a copy of the Old Testament written in the language spoken by the people who came from Abraham's family. It is called the Hebrew language. The first letter of the Hebrew alphabet looks like this (*I'll put it on the chalkboard*):

This letter is something like our *A*.

PUPIL 5: Looks crazy.

TEACHER: (*C——— is resentful of anything he has to read. I wonder, is he getting the services of a reading specialist? The teacher didn't say, and neither did his parents. I hate to admit I don't know whether his school has a specialist. I must look into that tomorrow. Will jot it down on my lesson plan sheet. I write: Ck. on C———, reading specialist??*)

PUPIL 1: Write some more Hebrew, please!

PUPILS (in chorus): Write some more!

TEACHER: I haven't learned how to write very many letters, but I'll do the next two. (*I'll write these from right to left.*)

אבנ

The second one is like our *B*, and the third one is something like our *G*. You notice that I wrote those from right to left. (*I'll point that out with a right-to-left gesture.*) This is just the opposite from the way we write. That is the way all Hebrew writing goes. So, does anyone have an idea how you would open this Hebrew Bible?

PUPIL 1: Would it be at the back?

TEACHER: Yes, since the writing goes from right to left, the pages go from back to front. (*They need to look at this for themselves. I'll take the time to pass it around.*)

Pupils look at Bible, pass it along, make a few remarks. Teacher follows the Bible from pupil to pupil.

TEACHER: But the Hebrew Bible wasn't written on sheets of paper as we write. It was written on long strips of pressed papyrus and rolled into scrolls. (*I'll show them how with a sheet of paper rolled from each end around two pencils, then explain.*)

See, the scroll would be wound on wooden pieces something like this paper on these pencils. It had to be rolled up at one end and unrolled at another as you read it.

At this point, the teacher showed a filmstrip on the Hebrew Old Testament. The pupils continued a discussion of it with the teacher until the end of this segment of their instruction.

What had the *teacher* learned from this period of work with his pupils? At least the following items were in his notes at the end of the day:

1. These third-graders remembered more about the word "covenant" (and Abraham and Moses) than I thought they would. Pleasant discovery!

2. They weren't quite ready to role-play as interpreters of the Bible, with their teacher taking the part of a visitor.

3. C—— needs lots of help with reading. (Right diagnosis?)

The teacher's notes, whether or not he recognized the fact, touched on the three general areas of self-improvement every teacher must pursue at his own pace:

— Knowledge of the subject matter, in sequential order (in this case, the Bible and its time line).

— Techniques for use in the classroom (in this case, inductive questioning, use of the chalkboard, use of a filmstrip — a mediated teacher).

— Personal knowledge of the pupils and their individual needs (as in the special case of C—— with his reading problem, if that was the actual reason for his reactions in the class period; the teacher's analysis seems likely).

Note this teacher's apparent determination to make contact with the public school concerning one of his pupils. More exchanges between church and school can occur in this way, as teachers in both confer and compare notes on individual children and their needs.

Indeed, all the church's teachers should visit nearby public school classes now and then, just to check the level at which pupils are presently working. The best time to visit is during a period or module in the field of social studies. These are the courses that compare most directly with the kind of classroom work the church must do — these and literature classes. It is in the social studies classes, particularly, that children learn to examine and debate issues — just as they should do in their church classrooms.

Teachers of adults in the church may profit from observing how college and university extension courses are conducted. Another possibility for getting ideas on teaching would be to visit some of the sessions conducted in private industrial and technical training programs.

OTHER RESOURCES

Local educational television stations also present opportunities for the volunteer teacher to observe classroom practice. Tuning in on classes occasionally can help to enlarge a teacher's vision of what can be accomplished in a short period of time and how a subject can be introduced and explored, then summarized at the end.

Teachers should not overlook the resources of public libraries, and especially of historical museums and other local institutions that offer special educational services. A splendid example of this type of assistance is the program of the Historical Society of Delaware.[16]

The Society delivers to public school classrooms many rare objects that illustrate periods of history the children are studying. The teacher is given background material on each artifact or piece of equipment, and the pupils are permitted to handle them — such objects as revolvers that "won the West," garments the pioneers made by hand, fans of ivory and silk from the Orient, looms, and early electrical appliances.

The response to this Delaware program has been enthusiastic. Children look forward to seeing and handling the concrete evidence of men's life in other times. This state historical society believes it should preserve not only antique objects but also significant materials that document more recent periods in American history. Churches may participate in its programs simply by asking.

Theological institutions often have large collections of items obtained on archaeological expeditions, and it would be helpful if they could be persuaded to put together similar exhibits for loan to church classrooms. The Delaware program would serve as an excellent prototype for such a venture. It would mean bringing Bible and church artifacts directly to the classroom rather than relying on expeditions for teacher and pupils, probably only to see things under glass.

This chapter has turned into a potpourri. It is meant to stimulate more thoughts in the same precise direction at which the whole book is aimed — toward the classroom. The point is that a teacher doesn't have to know everything at the start. Neither do we need to frighten him with a solemn charge to spend a certain number of hours in poring over curricular materials. What we should aim for is a gradual induction of this beginning teacher into the thrill of discovering things and sharing them with his pupils.

Teaching can become, for almost anyone willing to give it his best, something far more than a tedious duty to be performed. Instead, it can be a means to personal renewal and widened vision.

The volunteer teacher should be recruited with these words:

" We hope you'll enjoy your work, and that you won't hesitate to try fresh approaches as you discover them. We'll do everything we can to supply you with easily accessible resources. We'll spare nothing to support this terribly important thing we are asking you to do. Some things we can arrange to teach you in special training opportunities. But you, like all persons who have ever taught, will discover that no one can supply everything for you. At your own pace, as your interest in this job heightens, you will have to *teach things to yourself.*"

Who speaks such encouraging words to the teacher? Who supplies that unlimited support? In most parishes, no one does. That is the critical problem which, left long unsolved, will spell decline in the church's crucial ministry of teaching.

CHAPTER 7

OBSERVE — PRACTICE — TALK IT OVER

(Suggestions of a possible shape for the future in teacher education)

Most teacher education in the churches is *general.* Teachers are encouraged to go to a series of sessions in which pupils-in-general, techniques-in-general, and content-in-general are discussed. When the teachers return to their classrooms, they have difficulty in relating this generalized experience to the practical problems of what to do and say when they face living pupils. Too little attention has been given to the specifics — specifics that differ with every parish.

How, really, can a teacher be helped by others to improve in his work? Is there a better way than the usual teachers' institute or the typical "leadership" classes?

When we talk frankly with gifted teachers of long experience, we discover quite readily that they have learned best from *observing* other competent teachers. Nothing is remembered more vividly or is more influential toward changing a teacher's way of working than the simple experience of seeing how a good teacher operates in a normal church setting.

The young public school teacher entering upon a first job will usually find the routine quite different from anything encountered in the college of education. It will, therefore, be a natural first step to look up older, trusted friends in the profession and say, " Tell me, how would you handle my situation? " And at teachers' institutes or other gatherings planned for the teachers' professional growth, it will not be the formal seminars and plenary sessions that offer the greatest benefit. Rather, it will be the " sidebar " conversations held after hours and between times in the daily schedule. Here is where teachers facing similar assignments in comparable school systems with mutual problems can talk things over and share ideas. New, workable classroom techniques and new text materials are more often disseminated by word of mouth in this way than by formal programs launched for their introduction.

If teachers learn primarily from other, more experienced teachers, then the task before the decision makers in church education is to arrange for more opportunities to get teachers together in normal settings where ideas can rub off from one to another. While it would seem relatively easy to do so, one soon discovers the problems are not at all simple.

In the first place, the parish structure in most denominations seems to work against cooperation among congregations. There is a psychology of parish ministry that places high priority on self-sufficiency. Each pastor and each governing body in the localized setting tend to think of parish problems as *theirs* to solve. They must recruit, train, and dispatch their own leaders, with such resources as they can put together. Seldom do they seek out talent from neighboring congregations. And on the other side of the matter, seldom does a congregation's leaders consider how they might share their own talent with surrounding churches. The idea of interparish cooperation and mutual problem-solving through pooling of time, talents, and resources is virtually nonexistent. The independence of every parish militates against the exchange of talented individuals with good ideas. Often the church is more guilty than any other of today's permanent institutions when it comes to preserving parochial interests; the idea of a self-contained parish prevents a broader community of interests from emerging.

A teacher in Church A may struggle manfully with some classroom dilemma, totally unaware of a creative solution worked out by a teacher in Church B only a few blocks away. This happens over and over again because at present there is no structural provision, educationally speaking, for getting teachers into contact with one another. Not until sustained attention is given to new strategies for meeting this problem can we hope for general improvement in the education of teachers.

At present there are two basic ways of supplying educational services to parishes (by means of more than the printed page). One way is through professional personnel whose jobs entail itineration among the churches to organize and conduct educational meetings of various kinds as well as personal counsel to individual parish workers. The other way is through regional committees whose members represent the parishes; they plan and carry out regional training events to which all parishes are invited to send their personnel.

Neither of these ways of working is proving adequate. The professional itinerant usually has to cover too wide a territory. He cannot become closely acquainted with parish teachers, and he cannot maintain frequent contact with those persons he meets. He is here today, gone tomorrow, and his work is like a raindrop falling into a stream and creating ever so slight a ripple.

The committee approach breaks down because the members are persons already hip-deep in parish labors. Their work on the regional level must be minimal because of a lack of time in their personal schedules. Committees cannot find time for prolonged meetings, and they cannot, consequently, do a thorough analysis of regional problems. Nor can they devise programs that carry through from year to year, largely because of a swift turnover in their membership. Many fine events have been planned and carried out by regional committees, but these are one-shot affairs. They are, again, quite generalized in character in order to meet needs of a wide variety of parish settings. The result is a breakdown in strategy for providing maximum attention to the individual teacher's problems.

The itinerant professionals sometimes view their labors as administrative in character. Burdened by details that someone, somewhere must take on, they become truly directors and executive secretaries. This means even less time for teaching and direct service to the congregations in their regions. While they admit privately that they would like to be freed of their administrative roles, they continue to perform them. Their professional counsel is not sought, in many cases, largely because parish leaders either do not know what they have to offer or think of them as legmen and administrators. The image is hard to break down. It is harder when denominational committees tend to assign to these persons the administrative tasks others might perform just as easily.

CONSENSUS REQUIRED

If we concede that a way must be found to bring training opportunities closer to home for more teachers, and on a continuing basis, then the first way will surely be gaining a consensus in the church for more interparish co-operation.

If parishes could be grouped into clusters, or *development units,* with no more than eight churches in each one, the possibility would then be open for obtaining an educational *coordinator* to work among these churches in the strictly limited field of teacher education.

This coordinator, in either a full-time, professional role or on a part-time, volunteer basis, should be a teacher of outstanding caliber — a person whose first and lasting interest is in the upgrading of teacher competence. His job would be threefold:

1. He would locate, among the parishes in his unit, those teachers already doing a reasonably competent job; for these persons he would supply additional training and resources. Persons thus helped and encouraged would be the *master teachers* within the unit of parishes — at least one for each age level or grade.

2. Next, the coordinator would arrange, on a systematic basis, for the other teachers in the churches of his unit to visit the classrooms of the master teachers. Here they could *observe* good teaching in progress, from start to finish. And the teaching would not be a specially staged demonstration session conducted in abnormal circumstances. Instead, it would be the teaching that occurs regularly under normal parish conditions.

3. The coordinator would arrange for observing teachers to meet periodically with master teachers for talk-it-over sessions where their own problems of classroom practice would get a sympathetic, full-scale review.

Very few prototypes for such a system of teacher education are now in existence.[17] Theoretically, there should be no barriers to establishing such development units. The only problems are the practical ones of getting enough decision makers interested and motivated to take on such a plan, and then getting together the money to put it into effect. (Money is especially difficult to obtain in just those parts of the country where full-time, professional help is most critically needed.)

On a wider scale, the Arizona Experiment in Biblical Studies and Teaching, of The United Presbyterian Church in the U.S.A., conducted in 1965–1967, was an attempt to bring a coordinated teacher training effort closer to the parishes. In the first year of that two-year venture, nearly 50 percent of the volunteer teachers of approximately eighty parishes were involved in training events, most of which included at least one demonstration teaching session conducted by the Experiment's teacher-in-residence.

In the teaching demonstrations of the Experiment, parish children were taught from current curricular materials, in close-to-normal classroom settings. Teachers observed, took notes, and discussed the sessions at length afterward. Even so, there was a certain artificiality in these events. The teacher-in-residence lacked any previous acquaintance with the pupils, and the settings were at odd hours, publicized as unusual, and not followed up by sufficient personal counseling with the observing teachers. Still, the Experiment's most widely praised feature was the teaching demonstration. Participants said they recalled it more clearly than other sessions for which the teacher-in-residence was responsible. Often the volunteer teachers would say: " This was the first time I had ever actually seen someone else teach in the church. It was helpful to have such a chance."

Development units with coordinators at work in them would make it possible to multiply many times over this invaluable experience of visiting regular classrooms and observing competent teachers on the job.

Everyone with any experience in trying to promote regional training events for teachers knows what an uphill problem it gets to be. Publicity is mailed to ministers and key laymen of the parishes, and it may or may not be read and shared with interested persons. Even where vigorous effort goes into persuading people to attend, it is not unusual for a potential registrant to telephone at the last minute, " I'm sorry, but I find I can't go after all." Patterns of increased secularization in the society, more intense in some regions than others, often make it difficult to attract really gifted people for participation.

Far too frequently, the events themselves are hastily put together. Persons who go sometimes complain: " But I really didn't get anything out of it. It didn't seem to apply to *my* situation." Not enough time is allotted, in many instances, for dealing with real problems in the churches of the enrollees. Moreover, the participants sometimes hesitate, on such short acquaintance, to share their real needs with the leaders of the event. They do not wish to divulge their lacks or misgivings in a general, public session.

On the other hand, when an event has been adequately planned and successfully carried out, some of the teachers who gained fresh vision of their tasks will return to their churches only to find it virtually impossible to convey their new enthusiasms to fellow parish workers who did not attend. The discouraged, isolated participant will say: " I couldn't use the things I learned. No one seemed to understand what I wanted to do."

The end result of a regional event may, therefore, be only a fractional carry-over from its offerings into the teaching ministry of the particular churches. Another subtle but certain disadvantage of regional events is that their planners sometimes tend to think they have discharged an annual or semiannual obligation to the teacher education effort when they have " done " the school or the institute. That these events are only a small beginning and need sustained follow-up is a fact seldom faced realistically by the committees that set them up.

OBSERVATION A KEY

For just the reasons cited above, it seems imperative to come up with a personalized approach to teacher development that offers some prospect of bringing about changes in what actually transpires in the parish. Coordinators in development units would be able to supply this personal touch, taking teachers by the hand, figuratively speaking, and arranging for them to observe master teachers, to practice on their own, and to talk things over among themselves.

Observation of a practicing teacher should be preceded by some instruction on what to look for. Various observation " instruments " have been devised, but most of these are long and complicated. If an inexperienced observer has to keep in mind a lengthy checklist of items, he tends to become preoccupied with the paperwork and misses what he should be seeing — teacher-pupil relationships and the interplay of many factors more properly appreciated as a whole rather than as isolated items on an observation " sheet."

It is adequate for the volunteer teacher visiting a master

teacher's classroom to suggest that he consider three principal questions, with a few additional questions and directions in parentheses:

1. *What did the pupils appear to be learning?* (What are your ideas on *why* they learned it? If they didn't seem to learn, why do you think this was the case?)

2. *What did the teacher do?* (Would you have done what he did? Why, or why not? Be critical. If you have questions about the techniques of this teacher, feel free to ask them.)

3. *What do you think was the content of today's class session?* (Could you discern one or more main ideas the teacher hoped the pupils would grasp? What were they?)

If a separate chalkboard or easel is available, the coordinator should further summarize what the observer is to look for by writing these headings:

> Pupils —
> Teacher —
> Content —

When the visit is ended, and the observers meet to discuss what they have seen and heard, the coordinator should let these headings supply a skeleton for all the observations the teachers will have to offer. At first, the discussion will move very slowly because they will be thinking intently about what they have observed. From forty to fifty minutes is usually required to get a good discussion under way after a classroom visit.

The discussion should end with a suggestion that each observer try to employ in his own teaching one or more of the new ideas he has gleaned from his visit in the master teacher's classroom. A date should also be set for a time to compare notes on what happened. In this follow-up session, it may not be at all unusual for a teacher to say: "Honestly, I tried to use some of the ideas. They didn't work for me, and I don't know why."

At this point, the coordinator — himself a good analyst of classroom problems — gently inquires into the difficulties, gives pointers on what may have gone awry, and (if he feels it is necessary) arranges for an early return visit to the master teacher's room.

In order to help readers visualize how a development unit might operate, the following imaginary description is supplied:

Unit I is composed of Churches A through H, and these congregations range in size from 100 to 1,500 members. A full-time coordinator, a trained educator with good theological background, has been employed. He has an office in the largest of the eight churches, where he has benefit of the secretarial pool and other services that a larger congregation is able to provide.

The coordinator spent a number of weeks visiting with teachers in the eight congregations. Through observation and skilled information-gathering, he selected a corps of master teachers:

Nursery, Church E; kindergarten, Church B.

Grades 1–2, Church A.

Grades 3–4, Church D.

Grades 5–6, Church E.

Junior highs, Church H.

Senior highs, Church F.

Adults, Church A.

(Note that Churches C and G did not have persons of the master teacher caliber.)

On a typical class day (Sunday in this particular case),

the coordinator arranged for first- and second-grade teachers from Churches B, C, G, and H to visit the classroom of
Mrs. Alpha at Church A. Teachers from Churches F, D,
and E could not attend; they were, therefore, asked to do
so at another time.

With Mrs. Alpha's cooperation, the observers were able
to sit through an entire hour of instruction. Then they
spent an additional hour and a luncheon period discussing
their observations and reactions. Mrs. Alpha answered
questions, and the coordinator guided the discussion and
offered a few of his own observations.

Teachers from Churches B and H were especially interested in Mrs. Alpha's approach to musical instruction. She
had integrated it with other material, and her song sheets
had been neatly lettered by a skilled commercial artist
whom she had recruited for the task. They indicated that
they would try this approach in their own classrooms.

Ten days later, the coordinator called on these teachers
in Churches B and H, to find out how they were getting
along in their work. One said she couldn't find anyone to
print song sheets. The other had made the sheets herself
but was having difficulty figuring out when to use them
in relation to the remainder of her teaching plans. ("It
seemed so natural and easy for Mrs. Alpha, but I don't
think I understand how to fit things together as she
does.")

From these conversations, the coordinator was able to
supply specific help and encouragement. The two teachers did acquire Mrs. Alpha's technique.

In the course of thirty-nine weeks, the coordinator conducted twenty-six observation visits within Unit I and
held countless personal conferences with teachers in all
eight churches. There were special cooperative sessions

for making lesson plans and reviewing general content of curricular units.

ECUMENICAL PLANNING

Would it be necessary that all churches in a unit belong to one denomination? Not at all if an ecumenical arrangement could be worked out in a given area. Curricular materials among the major denominations vary considerably only in thematic arrangement and general format. Theological and doctrinal variations are not great enough to prevent widespread cooperation in teacher education efforts.

Ideally speaking, the coordinators in such a setup of development units should be able to meet periodically for sharing mutual concerns and comparing notes on how to be helpful to the classroom teacher. They and master teachers could profitably take part in special institutes where noted educators, curriculum specialists, theologians, and Bible scholars would help to keep them abreast of developments in all these fields.

To give them special status, denominations might consider naming the coordinators to regional committees on the ministry of teaching, restructuring these groups so that they would be composed primarily of persons serving in a coordinating function. This would bring into planning committees for beyond-the-parish activity the very persons in closest touch with working conditions in the parish classrooms.

Readers with an eye to the financial outlay required for a nationwide adoption of the development unit plan will be quick to conclude that millions of dollars would have to be spent. True enough, but not necessarily additional budget. There are already several thousand persons trained in church education whose time is devoted largely to recruiting and " directing," but whose abilities to evaluate and help to redirect the classroom performance of teachers are not being used. Large congregations should be willing to share their personnel with smaller churches in the vicinity. Present blocs of Christian education directors, if they were deployed in a coordinating capacity and relieved of the tedious minutiae now cluttering so many of their desks, could effect dramatic changes in the quality of the church's teaching. Why not enlarge the scope of their position and give them a chance to cross-ventilate the parishes with fresh ideas and master teacher exchanges?

THE MAJOR HURDLE

Money is not the major hurdle. The clergy and chief decision makers of the denominations are the barrier. They do not mean to be, but they are. As indicated in Chapter 1, their highly creative minds have not really been challenged by the problems and opportunities of the *teaching* ministry. For some strangely elusive reason, the subject simply has not been compellingly brought to their attention. Crises call for action. That the need for better teaching in our time is a crisis-type situation has not been stated so that people who could do something about it are caught up in the cause.

A possible reason why the church's educational leaders have not been able to command a wider hearing is their propensity for relying on the printed page, and filling the page with too many words. The readers of educational material feel bamboozled. They find it hard to wade through all the expansive paragraphs; the dramatic impact seems to be missing.

Neither more printing nor more speeches at denominational assemblies will do the job of arousing genuine interest in the teacher's role. Something different is called for.

Some major Protestant body should lead the way by discarding its national board or department of Christian Education and forming in its place a national Commission on the Ministry of Teaching.[18] This would put the spotlight on the word " teaching " and get the churches to thinking about it.

Then this venturesome denomination should go on to institute a national plan for inviting every clergyman into church classrooms, *as an observer,* for an eight-week period. He would observe and take notes on what was being taught — and how — at every age level from the nursery on up. He would compare what was being taught with the expectations of the curriculum writers. And he would attend at least two conferences with fellow clergy at which they would discuss their observations.

This procedure, so fully church-oriented, would not in itself be adequate. These men would also need to be sent to the public schools nearest to their parish buildings, to visit classes there. (Clergymen of Philadelphia have been systematic observers of police operations in that city. Why not systematic observers of teaching operations?) And prime questions to be asked would be these: How does the teaching in our churches compare, on the whole, with the quality of instruction offered the children in public education today? How do the classrooms compare? What would be a child's normal reaction if he were asked to compare these church and school classrooms?

Only by seeing for themselves are clergymen going to be captivated by the possibilities that the church is now passing by when it fails to train and support its teachers adequately. Only by seeing and hearing will they become aware of how our brightest youngsters are subjected to woefully inadequate church teaching — not altogether through the failure of curricular resources, but certainly as a consequence of poorly prepared teaching staffs.

Even the staff members of denominational agencies for education sometimes go for years without actually visiting church classes at all age levels. They make speeches about education, but they cannot pepper their speeches with current illustrations from the classroom. They haven't been in the classroom, that's why. These persons, especially chief administrators, should be the first to lead the pilgrimage back to the real scene of action in church education. The scene is wherever a teacher and pupils are at work, learning and thinking things through together.

Probably no denomination as a whole will ever undertake such a program of classroom observation by its clergy. But if the preceding paragraphs jog a few men to become intimately acquainted with the real situation educationally, they will be well worth the ink and the paper.

POSSIBLE MODELS

Certainly the denominations should be able, cooperatively, to undertake a national program for establishing *model classrooms.*

Not surprisingly, the volunteer teachers' early questions about working with their pupils have to do with simple matters of equipment and room arrangement. They are questions such as: " Should the pupils sit in a circle or around tables? Where should the teacher stand? or sit? Where do you keep supplies? What's the best place for the piano? Do we need a piano? Where should the chalkboard go? "

The curricular materials prepared by the churches usually treat these problems of room arrangement once over lightly. They take for granted that local decision makers will have done what is needful.

Poor utilization of wall space, faulty lighting, haphazard floor plans, bad acoustics — all these disadvantages that plague the average church classroom *can* be corrected, and without great expenditures. But to do so requires the advice of thoughtful teacher-planners. The kind of caring that goes into classroom arrangement must be of the same quality as that of a workshop designer or a kitchen planner.

Children who behave badly in a classroom of the church are sometimes reflecting unconsciously what the room itself seems to say, namely, that no one cares very much about what happens there. Dirt and useless objects seem to collect surprisingly fast in church buildings. It is not at all rare to discover debris-laden classrooms in a parish house that adjoins a magnificent nave, beautifully done up and cared for. Why does this happen?

There is great need for accessible model classrooms just as there is for master teachers who can be enlisted to share their talents. Only at the nursery and kindergarten levels has progress been achieved toward this end. The entry of many larger churches into the field of preschool weekday education has promoted an interest in ideal room arrangement and equipment for teaching the very young child. At older age levels, few churches have exercised similar attentive care.

Rooms nicely equipped and arranged ("rooms that teach," as some persons are fond of saying) should be a concrete reality in every community. If Methodists take the lead toward producing model classrooms, why should they not receive Presbyterian and Baptist counsel, and even financial aid? The models could then be visited by decision makers of all the surrounding parishes.

Such a program might have the effect of focusing attention upon this vital matter. Through visits and open houses, persons would be encouraged to borrow and adapt good ideas. The only possible outcome would be improved quality and efficiency.

Lest we give the impression that church equipment should be competitive on every count with public school material, it should be stated unequivocally that such elaborateness is not only impossible to achieve but also an unnecessary goal. The point is simply that the church's teaching calls for efficient use of space, adequate equipment, cleanliness, and order. And if six-year-olds are sitting in full-size chairs, their feet and legs hanging uncomfortably, and their heads craning over adult-sized tables, this situation needs correcting. (Incidentally, the use of sturdy wall-to-wall carpeting makes it possible for pupils to sit on the floor — a practice now common in progressive, experimental public schools.)

Model classrooms, nicely equipped and lighted, are especially desirable in low-income areas where the church's mission is partly to provide a place of cheerful environment in the midst of drab surroundings. A development unit plan of coordinating the church's teaching ministry might include plans whereby affluent congregations could help to furnish and rearrange the facilities of mission churches in such areas. The missions would be full participants in the units, and hence the sharing of resources would not be patronizingly undertaken; it would simply be a matter of lifting standards for a mutual ministry by all churches in the cluster.

WORLD STRATEGY

An ultimate consideration in the whole area of educational strategy should be the interrelatedness of all congregations throughout the world. The same problems of teacher-pupil involvement are present in every nation of the globe today. A number one priority in each new nation, as we well know, is education. The church of Jesus Christ faces challenges in helping to raise literacy levels, to improve people's health and nutrition, and to supply elementary instruction in the gospel. With good fortune having attended so many of the West's educational efforts, it is incumbent on our churches to share talents and ideas with those who have need to learn and assume roles of leadership in their own national development.

Fraternal workers and missionaries on furlough, as well as indigenous church leadership from other countries, should be able to share on an equal basis in the educational wealth of the American congregations. When these persons come to the United States, they are often feted at board and agency offices and given hasty tours of a few congregations. But the number of opportunities for them to pay close attention to the classroom and a teacher's skills is still quite limited.

The development unit idea, with master teachers and model classrooms, would be ideally suited to a worldwide dissemination of improved teaching techniques. Units might conceivably be related on a continuous personal basis to one or more overseas congregations. Through the World Council of Christian Education, a body that works earnestly to lift educational standards through mutual exchanges among national churches, it should be possible to do far more than we are now doing to encourage ecumenical involvement. It would be good for Americans in particular to learn of the great needs in many quarters for the most elementary kinds of curricular resources and educational equipment. But real knowledge of the overseas church is not likely to penetrate widely into our consciousness unless there is more teacher-to-teacher, personal exchange — brought about consciously by people who care. By no means can we assume that ecumenical involvement is complete if board secretaries exchange memoranda about it and attend one another's consultative conferences. It is the classroom teachers themselves who must be brought together, and in great numbers.

This final chapter, with its case for classroom observation and mutual exchanges among teachers, comes out right where we started at the beginning of Chapter 1.

Our claim is simple: The church's teaching ministry falters in our time. It does so because the decision makers of today have not sensed fully the scope of the crisis. They fail to list teacher education as a top priority.

Unless teachers are taught and foundations for teaching are renewed, unless massive support is forthcoming for improved classroom practice, the church itself will suffer grave reverses in years to come.

Already the signs can be read. Already the walls tremble as families begin to fall away from the American congregations. Will we give support to the *teacher* and stand by his side to help him share the Christian heritage? Failure to do so in new, imaginative ways will mean that we passed by our finest opportunity of the twentieth century.

NOTES

1. An instructive discussion on the need for classroom teachers to be involved at every stage in the design, testing, and dissemination of educational resources may be found in the pamphlet *Organizing New York State for Educational Change*, by Henry M. Brickell. (Published in 1963 at Albany, New York, by the State Education Department of New York.) See also Robert Heath's *New Curricula* (Harper & Row, Publishers, Inc., 1965).

2. For a brilliant analysis of the crucial issue of centralized vs. local planning, consult Peter F. Drucker's *Landmarks of Tomorrow* (Harper & Brothers, 1959).

3. For an excellent recent treatment of what is at stake in the inductive and deductive modes of thought, the reader is referred to *Two Modes of Thought*, by James Bryant Conant (Pocket Books, Inc., 1964). He contrasts the European preference for the deductive-theoretical and the American preference for the inductive-empirical.

4. The material that follows, down to the heading, "Getting Somewhere," is taken from a paper prepared by the author (unpublished) under the title "An Operational Proposal for . . . Teacher Training Design." This working paper is on file in the United Presbyterian Board of Christian Education, Philadelphia.

5. Full treatment of the inductive process of Biblical study may be found in Howard Tillman Kuist's *These Words Upon Thy Heart* (John Knox Press, 1947). The late Professor Kuist

continued the work of an earlier teacher of the inductive method, Wilbert Webster White. Today, Prof. Vartan D. Melconian, McCormick Theological Seminary, Chicago, is a leading advocate of this method of Bible teaching.

6. A graduate student at Princeton Theological Seminary, William Chapman, did some interesting research into this classification of teachers in the spring of 1966. He labeled the author's types the Bowman Inventory and devised a questionnaire for determining where a small sampling of New Jersey teachers would be classified as to their preferences. His unpublished paper suggests that the Inventory may need revisions and that it is "too neatly descriptive." His quite limited research, however, did not invalidate the Inventory. The author believes that this questionnaire could have been designed to reveal more about the teachers than it did.

7. See *Opening Doors*, April–June, 1966, p. 51 (Board of Christian Education of The United Presbyterian Church in the U.S.A., Philadelphia).

8. See *Discovery*, April–June, 1966, p. 50 (Board of Christian Education of The United Presbyterian Church in the U.S.A., Philadelphia).

9. A most helpful book on the subject of Biblical analogy is *The Use of Analogy in the Letters of Paul*, by Herbert M. Gale (The Westminster Press, 1964).

10. The lecturer was James E. Russell, Secretary, Educational Policies Commission, National Education Association, at the annual Department of Audio Visual Instruction convention, San Diego, California, April, 1966.

11. Through the years, *Saturday Review* has published numerous essays and interviews reflecting these thoughts among key physical scientists.

12. The "mediated teacher" concept was stressed in an address by Prof. Robert Heinich, University of Southern California, at the 1966 DAVI convention, San Diego.

13. Related by the project director, Rev. Edward A. White, at United Presbyterian National Christian Education Staff Conference, Atlantic City, New Jersey, March, 1966.

14. For good, simplified chronologies, see Barbara Smith's *Young People's Bible Dictionary* (The Westminster Press,

1965), p. 15; and Winthrop S. Hudson's *The Story of the Christian Church* (Harper & Brothers, 1958), pp. 102–103.

15. An excellent listing, with brief descriptions of each technique, is offered by Dorothy B. Fritz, in her *Ways of Teaching* (published for the Cooperative Publication Association by The Westminster Press, 1965). She divides classroom techniques into those which are teacher-centered (such as lectures, directed study, etc.) and those which require a maximum of pupil participation (such as role-playing and notebook work).

16. Data and descriptions supplied by Dale Fields, the Society's director and originator of the program. (Address: Delaware Historical Society, Wilmington, Del.)

17. The development unit idea is adapted in part from the work of Henry M. Brickell, New York, as outlined in *Organizing New York State for Educational Change* (*op. cit.*). Mr. Brickell did his research under a Ford Foundation grant (Fund for the Advancement of Education).

18. When the name "Board of Foreign Missions" no longer did justice to the concept of ecumenical mission, the United Presbyterian Church replaced it with a Commission on Ecumenical Mission and Relations. The change was hailed by Dr. John Mackay as "linguistically inevitable." Perhaps the time has come in the church's history when the idea of a Board of Christian Education (or Department, or simply Board of Education) no longer is adequate for those denominations committed to a teaching ministry. Hence the suggestion, Commission on the Ministry of Teaching.